THE ALPINE PASS ROUTE
SWITZERLAND

The final approach to the Bunderchrinde crosses a slope of bare scree

THE ALPINE PASS ROUTE SWITZERLAND

BY

KEV REYNOLDS

CICERONE PRESS
MILNTHORPE, CUMBRIA

ACKNOWLEDGEMENTS

I am grateful to Franz Blum and Caroline Gut at the Swiss National Tourist Office for their generous assistance during the research for this book. My thanks are also due to Jim Reville of Sherpa Expeditions who sent me out on an initial exploration of the Alpine Pass Route, and to those who shared that first trek with me; especially Bart Jordans and Anne and John Shipley whose laughter matched the sunshine. For the full traverse it was good to have the company once again of Nigel Fry, as well as the undiminished enthusiasm of Brian and Aileen Evans who brought a new dimension to the walk. My old friend Roland Hiss, who has trekked just about everywhere, grabbed a wet day with us too and added his own brand of sunshine. With such companions, who cares about the rain? Brian Evans has added much to this guidebook with his sketches. I am delighted to benefit from his talent and his friendship. Thanks Brian, I hope this brings back some good memories.

Grateful thanks too, go to Bruno and Tilli Baer for marvellous Swiss hospitality both before and after the walk. They have a great way of turning strangers into friends. But as ever, my greatest debt is to my ever-patient wife who stayed at home and paid the bills while I strode across the mountains with notebook and camera. One day we'll return to walk the route together.

Kev Reynolds

Cicerone Press Guides by the same author
Walks & Climbs in the Pyrenees
The Wealdway & The Vanguard Way
Walking in Kent
The South Downs Way & The Downs Link
The Cotswold Way
Walks in the Engadine - Switzerland
The Valais
The Jura (with R B Evans)

Forthcoming
The Bernese Alps
Ticino
Central Switzerland

CONTENTS

INTRODUCTION

There's immense satisfaction to be gained in undertaking a long journey across a mountain landscape. There's the daily challenge, of course - reaching the summit of a pass that has occupied most of a morning to reach to be greeted by a panorama of unimagined beauty, with peaks and ridges on a far horizon that will lure you on in the days to come. And when at last you gain those distant ridges, having unravelled all the mysteries in between, you then exchange them for yet new horizons, new mysteries, new scenes of wonder and enchantment; conjuring dreams then setting those dreams into moulds of reality, and as you do so creating memories to cherish in the years ahead.

A long journey across a mountain landscape can be a great source of satisfaction and untold pleasure. And when that journey traverses an Alpine country as lovely as Switzerland, and when that landscape consists of mountains as full of charisma and grace as are the Wetterhorn, Eiger, Mönch, Jungfrau, Gspaltenhorn, Blümlisalp and Les Diablerets, then the journey may be seen as one of magnetic appeal and with magnificent rewards for those who complete it.

Such a journey is that travelled by walkers along the Alpine Pass Route.

✳ ✳ ✳

I first walked some of the APR, without realising it, nearly twenty-five years ago, and over the years I've returned several times to walk other sections - again without realising it. Then, rather fortuitously, I was sent on a journalistic assignment to cover a commercial trek across the central section of the APR from Altdorf to Lauenen.

It proved to be one of the finest, most enjoyable walks I'd ever undertaken, and as soon as it was over I determined to return again to Switzerland at the earliest opportunity in order not just to repeat it, but to complete the whole route from Sargans to Montreux. This turned out to be every bit as magical as I'd hoped - and then some. The Alpine Pass Route, I discovered, is not only one of the classic walks of the Alps, it will stand comparison with almost any other long walk in Europe.

7

THE ALPINE PASS ROUTE

The Alpine Pass Route traverses Switzerland from east to west; from the ancient town of Sargans on the borders of Liechtenstein, to Montreux on the shores of the Lake of Geneva. It covers some 325 kilometres of mountain and valley, and crosses sixteen passes with an accumulation of almost 18,000 metres of height-gain in fifteen stages.

And what stages these are!

Every one lives up to its promise. Each day begins with the prospect of wandering for hour after hour through valleys full of riches - wild flowers, streams, crags, waterfalls, cowbells and birdsong, isolated farms and haybarns, pasture and woodland - walled by great mountains set to catch your breath with sheer wonder at their scale and variety. Some of the valleys sparkle with tarns. Some are draped with glaciers curling off the mountains; others crusted with moraine deposits left by the ice sheets of a thousand years and more ago. Some are gentle, pastoral swathes - great grass-blanketed hammocks slung between the mountains. Some have been scoured into deep U-shaped trenches by the ice, like that of the Weisse Lütschine, the valley of Lauterbrunnen; an astonishing sight no matter how often one has seen it.

Every pass is a pass worth aiming for and worth reaching. Each one is different. Each has its own special attributes; from the remote, slender crest of the Richetli to the broad, tourist-thronged Kleine Scheidegg; from the narrow, rocky cleft of the Bunderchrinde to the open grassy saddle of the Blattipass with its incredible vista that encompasses so many of the giants of the Bernese Oberland.

And it's not only the valleys and passes that make this route so memorable, but the villages along the way too. These also add their own very special character to the journey. Switzerland, of course, is not a wilderness land and the little clusters of habitation are as much a part of the landscape as are the snow-capped peaks and glaciers. So you come down at the end of a day to such delightful villages as Weisstannen and Elm, to Griesalp or Gsteig. Flower-decked villages, bright at balconies that gaze on the mountains you've been rubbing your nose against all day long. Villages set in a pastoral land where men and women toss the hay with long-handled forks, or drape the newly-cut grass to dry on cross-frames of timber, so that from a distance the hillsides seem to be peopled by battalions of hairy dwarfs.

There are marmots in the wild inner recesses of the upper valleys, and chamois among the screes. There are deer in the forests, buzzards in the sky and a million crickets buzzing like fury in the grasses at your feet.

But it is to the mountains that the Alpine Pass wanderer sets his eyes, and it is prospects of the mountains that first capture the imagination for such a walk.

At first, in the east where you rise out of Sargans, the peaks are little-known and scantily dressed in snow, yet their scale is perfect for an introduction. They do not appear forbidding. They have a certain benevolence, clad as they are with forested skirts, and it is right that they should lead you gently to larger sport only when you've got into your stride and adjusted to Alpine proportions. Then there will be more than enough to satisfy your longing. There's the Tödi and Titlis, for example, and plenty of their neighbours spreading shawls of snow and ice, their walls plunging to valleys green and lush with flowers. Then you enter the Bernese Alps, and at once stroll beneath the rock climbers' slabs of the Engelhörner on the way to Grosse Scheidegg, where you rub shoulders with the Wetterhorn which keeps watch, of course, over Grindelwald.

The Bernese Oberland is known to mountain lovers far and wide, the fabled tryptich of Eiger, Mönch and Jungfrau recognised at once even by those who have never been in their shadow before. To walk below them is a special privilege on a day that takes you from Grindelwald to Alpiglen, to Kleine Scheidegg and the Wengernalp where for a century and more thousands of mountain wanderers have gazed in awe at the avalanches rolling off the Jungfrau. Then across the Lauterbrunnen valley where the Breithorn smiles down from its airy perch; the Gspaltenhorn with its monstrous long ridge, and to the huge massif of the Blümlisalp rising from Oeschinensee's deep and tranquil well.

West of Kandersteg the mountains fall away a little shyly, but the Wildstrubel shines its pristine snows at Adelboden. After this there's the Wildhorn and the great block of Les Diablerets marking the western extremity of the Oberland. That leaves only the Vaudois mountains to explore. Unsung they may be, but they're utterly delightful for all their comparative obscurity and with some superb valleys cutting between them.

From start to finish the Alpine Pass Route has all the scenic variations you can possibly wish to experience within the compass of a mountain environment.

* * *

It would be wrong, however, to suspect that the APR is the sole preserve of the hardened walker. Such a route in wilderness country would indeed be so, but Switzerland makes things easy for mountain trekking and backpacking becomes unnecessary in a land where there are villages with food shops on practically every stage, where there are hotels, gasthofs and simple *matratzenlagers* (dormitories) liberally scattered along the route, and where there are transport options that effectively reduce any problems that could occur through bad weather, injury or just plain weariness.

Of course, one could tackle the APR as a long-distance backpacking route, carrying a tent and camping wild (with discretion) or on campsites where they occur. You can walk every step of the way and carry all the necessities of food and accommodation as though there were no alternatives available. And there can be a great deal of satisfaction in doing so.

But not everyone will be tempted to do this, and the APR is far too good a route to have it restricted to such an attitude of travel. There will be many walkers perfectly capable of tackling each individual pass but who would be daunted by prospects of backpacking, yet given the wonderful assortment of lodgings available, plus the possibility of easing a particularly long or wet day by the use of a Postbus, funicular or cable-car, would find that the Alpine Pass Route suddenly becomes perfectly feasible. This guidebook has been written with such walkers very much in mind.

There is no marked route of the APR. True, an abundance of signposts and waymarks accompany every stage with characteristic Swiss efficiency, but nowhere will you find a sign announcing the existence of the Alpine Pass Route as such. It will follow, therefore, that the way is open to interpretation. But whichever assortment of passes you choose to cross between Sargans and Montreux, end to end the route will require at least fifteen days of consistent walking. Some of the days are in the order of eight, nine or even ten hours long. That's walking time and does not take into account rest stops, photographic interruptions etc. However, the longest of these stages may be broken by the use of an intermediate lodging - maybe not in a village, but in a remote mountain inn (*gasthof*) or a farm with an outhouse converted to dormitory accommodation specifically designed with walkers or climbers in mind. Where these occur a note is given in the text, together with the approximate amount of time required to reach it from the beginning of that stage, so you can decide almost before you set out just how far you intend to walk on any particular day.

Similarly, mention is made wherever transport options occur. On one or two stages a spell of road-walking becomes necessary and you might decide to conserve your energies and take a bus over these sections. Likewise where cable-cars, chair-lifts and funiculars could be taken to facilitate the ascent of a steep section, information is offered to allow you to decide whether or not to take advantage of it.

Walking the APR should be an enjoyable and unforgettable experience. If that enjoyment is to be threatened in any way, either by bad weather, an over-long stage that brings on exhaustion, or by sore feet through tramping too far along a tarmac road, then alternatives are there for you to consider. No-one should feel reticent about doing so; the only rules to the game of mountain walking are those set by each individual rambler.

✳   ✳   ✳

Not everyone tempted to tackle the route will feel inclined to commit fifteen days of their holiday to an end to end route without the occasional day off. The following suggestions are therefore given for breaking the route into two separate walking holidays of a fortnight each.

Walk 1: Sargans to Lauterbrunnen (Stages 1-8, using Alternative Stage 4) with days off in Engelberg, Meiringen, Grindelwald and Lauterbrunnen to either rest or explore further.

Walk 2: Lauterbrunnen to Montreux (Stages 9-15) with days off in Lauterbrunnen, Kandersteg, Adelboden, Lauenen and/or Gsteig. Each of these villages will repay a wider exploration of the surrounding mountains.

Whilst it would seem a little churlish to choose just one section of this scenically spectacular route as being the best of all, if you can only manage one part of the APR and are unable to consider spending more than two weeks on it, I would suggest tackling the central, Bernese Oberland, section with a preface beginning at Altdorf. In two weeks you could have a magnificent walk journeying between Altdorf (Stage 5) and Gsteig (Stage 13) and still take time off in Grindelwald, Lauterbrunnen and Kandersteg. But you'd also be missing some fine country elsewhere. (One or two commercial trekking companies organise walking holidays along much of this central part of the route, and are an option worth considering.)

GETTING THERE AND BACK AGAIN

Travel to Switzerland is relatively easy. Regular flights by Swissair between the U.K. and Switzerland are operated in conjunction with British Airways. Scheduled routes are from London (Heathrow) to Geneva, Basle and Zürich. Services also operate from Manchester, Birmingham and Dublin. Flight information may be obtained from Swissair, Swiss Centre, New Coventry Street, London W1V 4BJ, or from British Airways, 75 Regent Street, London W1. Dan-Air services operate between London (Gatwick) and Bern or Zürich.

Air services from North America fly to Geneva and/or Zürich from Boston, Chicago, Los Angeles, Montreal and New York. Those airlines that maintain a routing across the Atlantic are Swissair, Trans World Airlines, Air Canada and Pan American. Swissair have offices in Atlanta, Boston, Chicago, Dallas, Hartford, Houston, Los Angeles, Miami, Minneapolis, Clifton (NJ), New York, Philadelphia, San Francisco and Washington DC, and in Canada at Montreal and Toronto.

Zürich is the most convenient airport for reaching Sargans, by which it is connected with a fast rail link. Zürich is also accessible from Montreux at the end of the APR, but usually via Lausanne. Geneva airport is on a more direct rail link with Montreux.

By rail the journey from Britain to Switzerland is straightforward. Either take the superfast TGV from Paris to Lausanne, and then change for Zürich and Sargans, or use the service Calais-Basle-Zürich-Chur which stops at Sargans.

Unless you have someone who will look after your car in Switzerland whilst you embark on the long walk, it is unlikely that motoring from Britain will be relevant. However for those who wish to travel by road, there is now an autoroute across France from Calais as far as the approach to Strasbourg. It is a fast route, but be prepared to pay several tolls on the way. From Strasbourg you can cross into Germany and take the autobahn route to Basle. Alternatively, linking autoroutes make a fast crossing possible through Belgium, Luxembourg and Germany, with a spur to Basle for entry into Switzerland, without paying any tolls. It should be noted, however, that a special annual motorway tax is levied on all motorists entering Switzerland who wish to use the Swiss motorway system.

ACCOMMODATION

On a walk like this, where day-to-day conditions in the mountains can dictate whether or not it will be possible to cross a pass, or when you can have an 'off day' that will throw a neatly-planned schedule to the winds, it is sometimes difficult to predict exactly where you will be at the end of any given stage. Booking accommodation in advance can therefore be unwise. Flexibility is the key-word to any long distance walk, and Switzerland is perhaps the best country in the world for wanderers to enjoy a flexible attitude with some degree of certainty of finding overnight lodging at the close of the day. Practically every village along the Alpine Pass Route provides a choice of accommodation, and between villages there will often be found a gasthof or *matratzenlager* offering an overnight's rest in a secluded position. Outline details are given in the text wherever accommodation is to be found along the route. It is not possible to give precise information in this guidebook, but up-to-date lists of hotels, gasthofs etc. in specific areas may be obtained from the Swiss National Tourist Office.

Weighed against the price of an organised holiday, the cost of walking the APR and using a combination of hotels and *matratzen-lagers* need not be overly expensive. It is perhaps worth mentioning that an overnight in a medium-grade Swiss hotel will be less costly than in a similar standard of hotel in Britain. *Matratzenlagers* are considerably cheaper, but you share a dormitory and often use communal washing facilities. Walkers used to staying in Youth Hostels will find that private *matratzenlagers* compare favourably, and those experienced by me and my companions when walking this route proved indeed to be memorable lodgings. One had excellent kitchen facilities in which we could prepare our own food, and another was in a timber-creaking traditional Oberland farm with the most outstanding views from its doorway.

There are also a few Youth Hostels along the route. These are mentioned in the heading to each stage where they occur, but check the International Youth Hostel Handbook (or the Swiss Youth Hostel Guide) for up-to-date information. If you plan to use hostels whilst in Switzerland, it is worth taking out membership of your home YHA in advance of your travels, as it is more expensive to join an overseas organisation. Membership of your domestic Youth Hostels Association is recognised internationally.

There is only one mountain hut on the route: the Blümlisalphütte a few metres above the highest pass, the Hohtürli on Stage 10. Owned by the Blümlisalp Section of the Swiss Alpine Club, it occupies a stunning position, and recent refurbishments have made it an extremely comfortable lodging. An overnight there would be rather expensive (reduced fees only for members of an Alpine Club which enjoys a reciprocal arrangement), but the experience would no doubt more than outweigh the cost.

As for camping, official campsites are to be found along the route at Elm, Engelberg, Grindelwald, Lauterbrunnen, Kandersteg, Adelboden, Lenk, Gsteig and Montreux. Off-site camping is officially discouraged in Switzerland since grasslands form a valuable part of the agricultural economy, and although it would not be beyond the bounds of possibility for individual backpackers to find a discreet corner of an alp for a single night's stay, it would be irresponsible for the guidebook writer to indicate likely sites. Suffice to say that in my experience, each time I have needed a pitch and there was no official campsite available, every farmer approached has readily agreed to my request and made me most welcome. Four of us were once even offered the free use of the garden of a village gasthof for our tents - even though there were rooms available for rent inside!

Should you camp off-site, please be discreet, take care not to foul water supplies, and pack all litter away with you.

WEATHER

It has to be said that the mountain areas traversed on the Alpine Pass Route are among the wettest in all of Switzerland, the Bernese Alps in particular, facing north as they do, attracting the bad weather which periodically sweeps in across north-western Europe. Most summers will be marked by days of low cloud and rain, while the region is also affected by the warm Föhn winds which blow through the north-south valleys. In the Haslital (crossed on Stage 6) for example, the Föhn is experienced on some 79 days of the year.

Even during the very height of summer precipitation on some of the passes crossed by the APR can be in the form of snowfall while rain falls in the lower valleys. Temperatures vary enormously, too.

However, that is only one side of the picture. The other is one of long summer days of clear skies and sparkling sunshine, the sort of days you dream about when making plans. Probably a mixture of good and bad is about as much as you can expect, therefore no-one should allow prospects of possible bad weather to deter them from making plans to walk the Alpine Pass Route. Go prepared for the worst, and hope for the best.

An up-to-date weather report may be obtained by telephone. The number to dial is 162.

The earliest time to consider setting out on the APR is the beginning of July. Earlier than this and one should expect snow and possibly ice creating hazards on some of the loftiest of passes, while even in mid-July you can experience soft melting snow in places. July of course is quite magical for the wild flowers that carpet the hillsides, although the lower valley meadows will largely have been shorn of their late-spring and early summer flowers. August is often damp, while early September is probably the optimum period in which to tackle the route. By the middle of September autumn is making itself felt and nights will be growing cold. The occasional dusting of snow should not be unexpected.

NOTES FOR WALKERS

The rewards waiting those who tackle the Alpine Pass Route are almost limitless. There is something in the Alps for practically every taste, and as many pleasures to be found in the lowest valley as on the loftiest pass. Each level has its own spice, its own indefinable charm. Much of the pleasure of the walk, of course, comes from the enormous variety of scenery along the way, and if you set out with an eye for the views, for the flowers and shrubs in the meadows, the multi-pat-terned rocks beside the path, for the birds of the air and the creatures of scree-slope and pasture, for the crystal clarity of the streams and tarns and the dark mystery of the forests, you'll never suffer a dull day. Enjoy the farms and barns and geranium-bright villages; the fragrance of new-mown hay and the labours of the men and women at work in the meadows. Enjoy the steep uphill as much as the downward sloping pathway; greet days of wind and wildness as readily as you do those of balmy sunlight. For each is an expression of the mountain world, and an integral part of the walker's experience. Let every experience become indelibly etched in your mind and you'll return home with riches untold.

Careful preparation before setting out on a long walk is almost too obvious to require statement here. However, having accompanied walking parties on many occasions - in the Alps and elsewhere - it is apparent that a surprising number of people embark on a walking holiday with little more preparation than would be required of passengers on a coach tour. As a consequence the first few days become an ordeal, and not the enjoyable experience the trek ought to be. With a little thought and a small amount of effort required to prepare for the Alpine Pass Route, the results will pay dividends.

There is probably no better preparation for a walking holiday than walking. The best exercise for mountain walking is walking over hills. Take a weekend or two to explore on foot the countryside near your home; a few evenings' brisk exercise will help tone the muscles and get the body and legs into shape in readiness for the first stage of the APR. Carry a rucksack with a few belongings in it to help your shoulders grow accustomed to the weight. If on the first day out from Sargans your lungs and legs scream a complaint, then you've probably not done enough to get fit, and the crossing of the Foopass will not be as enjoyable as it deserves. The first pass is every bit as important as the highest or the last, the first day out ought to be as enjoyable as any and every other. With forethought it can be.

The next point to consider, having prepared mind and body, is that of equipment, the choice of which can make or mar a walking holiday. Boots, quite naturally, are of prime importance. They should be comfortable and well-fitting and broken-in before embracing the Alps. Lightweight boots will ensure you arrive less weary at your day's destination than the more traditional and heavier variety.

There is a wide variation in terrain to be experienced, from steep screes to smooth plates of water-splashed rock, from tarmac roads to dusty valley tracks, from snow patches to boggy meadows. Boots should therefore protect feet and ankles from an assortment of obstacles, and the soles should have thick cleats (Vibram or similar) to afford grip.

Gaiters are favoured by some walkers. They will protect your lower legs against snow or long wet grass. The shorter, ankle variety (sometimes known as *stop tous*), are a useful alternative. They help to keep small stones and snow out of your boots, but are not high enough to protect the legs.

Good waterproofs are essential, not just as protection against rain or snow, but just as importantly will double as windproofs; cagoule and overtrousers made of one of the 'breathable' materials such as Goretex are recommended. Remembering that some of the passes to be crossed are over 2,500 metres a warm pullover and/or pile jacket should also be taken, as should gloves and a balaclava or other woollen hat.

If one needs to be prepared to face cold and wet weather, the extremes of dazzling sun and unshaded heat can also cause problems. Sun cream (factor 6 or stronger) and sunglasses should be part of every APR walker's equipment.

A first aid kit is essential; and water bottle, compass, headtorch and spare batteries, whistle and maps should also be taken. Keep spare clothing in a large plastic bag inside your rucksack.

If you plan to camp along the way, then you will clearly need a large rucksack to hold your tent, sleeping bag, insulation mat, cooker and billies. Gaz cannisters are readily available in many villages on the route, and at some of the official campsites. For campers using multi-fuel stoves, petrol can be bought at one or two filling stations in villages en route. Engelberg has a handy supply. Meths and paraffin can be bought in Kandersteg.

Campers will find it unnecessary to carry large amounts of food with them as there are plenty of villages with food stores to pass through. Again, a note is given in the text when these are to be found. However, on occasion it will be essential to carry food for a couple of days. (Most shops are closed on Sundays, and some close for half a

day either during the week, or on Saturdays.) Where this is necessary, careful buying can save carrying too many heavy items. Most
food stores stock packet soups, packets of *rösti* (potato for frying) and
also packets of some ready-prepared vegetables. These are not
dehydrated, but moist and tasty, and are sometimes dressed in a type
of French-dressing sauce. They are light to carry, easily packed in a
rucksack and quick to prepare.

A word about drinking water in the mountains. Most of the
streams seen tumbling down the hillsides should be safe enough to
drink from, unless there is an alp above where cattle or sheep may be
grazing - or where there is habitation in some form or another. I have
never personally experienced any problems from drinking directly
from mountain streams, but one should in any case treat all such
water sources with a degree of caution. Perhaps the safest course is
to top up water bottles only at village supplies or from those hewn-
out log troughs that are frequently found in valleys and pasture-
lands. They are filled by spring-fed pipes and the gushing fountain
should be perfectly safe for drinking.

One of the special features of mountain walking in the more popular
parts of Switzerland is the frequency with which one comes across
the possibility of refreshment. There are little restaurants, mountain
inns and farms doubling as restaurants in idyllic and seemingly
remote situations on a number of stages of the Alpine Pass Route.
Where these occur a note has been given in the text. On some days
your travelling time will be almost doubled if you give in to the
temptation to rest at every one! But in order to make the most of the
APR experience, and to gain some of the 'local colour' it's no bad
thing to stop now and then for a drink and, maybe, a bite to eat.
However, avoid alcoholic drinks until the day's walking is over, as
they will do little for your thirst. On warm, bright days I can
thoroughly recommend iced tea. This is, in my opinion, the most
thirst-quenching drink available. It is also the cheapest. On cold,
damp days, a bowl of steaming coffee or soup goes down well. At
lunch times, it is tempting to buy a platter of *bratwürst* and *rösti* (large
fried sausage served with a speciality based on fried potato). Almond

pastries are another local delicacy worth trying if you've an appetite that needs to be satisfied temporarily.

✳   ✳   ✳

On all but the last two days of the walk the route travels across German-speaking Switzerland. After Gsteig French dominates. But although the non-linguist may have difficulty in conversing with the occasional farmer or chamois hunter met upon the way, English is widely understood in most places and will certainly be spoken at campsites, hotels and gasthofs.

PATHS AND WAYMARKS

Most of the paths that make up the Alpine Pass Route have been in use for centuries by farmers, traders and huntsmen going about their daily business - from alp to alp, or from one valley to the next, or up onto a ridge where chamois might be spotted. Only in comparatively recent times have they come under the umbrella of care of either local communes or the various cantonal sections of the Swiss Footpath Protection Association *(Schweizerische Arbeitsgemeinschaft für Wanderwege)*.

Nowadays, footpaths in Switzerland fall under two headings: the *Wanderweg* and the *Bergweg*. A *Wanderweg* is a path that either remains in the valley itself, or runs along the hillside at a modest altitude. These are well maintained and are more gently graded than the *Bergweg*. They are waymarked with yellow paint flashes. Yellow metal signposts containing the names of major landmark destinations, such as a village, pass, lake, alp or footpath junction, are located in a number of prominent places. The nearest point is shown at the top, the more distant destination at the bottom, with intermediate points mentioned in between. Distances are indicated not in kilometres, but in hours *(Stunden)* and/or minutes *(Mins)*. A white plate between the direction boards contains the name and altitude at that point.

A *Bergweg* is a mountain path that ventures higher and is generally more demanding than a *Wanderweg*. These paths will usually be steeper, rougher, more narrow and sometimes fading if not in regular use. They explore the more remote regions of the mountains and are waymarked with red-white-red paint flashes. Signposting is similar to that for a *Wanderweg*, except that the outer sections of the finger post will be painted red and white. There may well be an occasional cairn to offer additional route-finding aid where the path has faded away or crosses a boulder slope, and in the event of low cloud obscuring the onward route it is essential to study the area of visibility with great care before venturing on to the next paint flash or stone-built cairn.

For the most part the footpaths adopted by the APR are clear and obvious, and waymarking is exemplary.

SAFETY IN THE MOUNTAINS

Although the APR is well signposted and there are working farms and villages strung along the route, there are several remote sections where an accident could have serious repercussions. Mountains contain a variety of objective dangers for the unwary and the long distance walker should be prepared to cope with any hazards that arise.

Plan each day's walk carefully. Study the route outline, the amount of height to be gained and time required to reach your destination. Make sure that you have enough hours in which to cross the day's pass and descend to the safety of the next valley, or to a place where a night's lodging can be had, before nightfall. Carry a few emergency food rations and a first aid kit. Know how to read both a map and compass, and watch for signs of deteriorating weather. Never be too proud to turn back if it is safer to do so than to continue in the face of an incoming storm.

In the unhappy event of an accident, stay calm. Should the party be large enough to send for help whilst someone remains with the injured member, make a careful written note of the exact location where the injured can be found. If there is a mountain hut or farm nearby, seek assistance there. If a valley habitation is nearer, find a telephone and dial 01 383 11 11. This calls out the Swiss Air Rescue - *but should only be used if absolutely essential.*

The international distress call is a series of six signals (either blasts on a whistle, or flashes by torch after dark) spaced evenly for a minute, followed by one minute's pause, then repeated with a further six signals. The reply is three signals per minute followed by a minute's pause.

Remember, there is no free rescue service in Switzerland, and no free hospital treatment. Emergencies will be extremely expensive. Specialist mountain insurance companies frequently advertise in the climbing press, and some standard holiday insurance policies can often be extended to include mountain walking in the Alps. But do check the small print for certain exclusion clauses, and make sure the cost of rescue (if required) is covered. Be insured, and be cautious.

RECOMMENDED MAPS

The *Landeskarte der Schweiz* (L.S.) series of maps that cover the Alpine Pass Route are works of art that will breed excitement in the heart of any map enthusiast. Open any sheet and a picture of the country immediately leaps from the paper. By clever use of shading, contours and colouring, the line of ridges and rock faces, the flow of glaciers and streams, the curve of an amphitheatre, the narrow cut of a glen, the expanse of a lake and the forest cover of a hillside all announce themselves clearly. They are a source of inspiration prior to setting out, and a real pleasure to use in the mountains.

At the head of each stage of the walk a note is given as to the recommended map to use. In every case I have chosen the 1:50,000 series, as this should be perfectly adequate. Greater detail should not be required, bearing in mind the route descriptions given in the text of this guidebook, plus the superb waymarking on the ground.

Eight sheets in all are required (including two double sheets) to cover the full route. They are summarised below:

No. 237	Walenstadt (Stage 1)
247	Sardona (Stage 2-3)
246	Klausenpass (Stage 3, 4, 5 & Alternative Stage 4)
245	Stans (Stage 5-6)
255	Sustenpass (Stage 6)
5004	Berner Oberland (Stage 7, 8, Alternative Stage 8, 9,10)
5009	Gstaad-Adelboden (Stage 11, 12, Alternative Stage 12, 13, 14)

262   Rochers de Naye (Stage 15)
Addresses of map suppliers are given in Appendix A.

USING THE GUIDE

A brief word of explanation about this guidebook. Distances are given throughout in kilometres and metres. Heights quoted are metric too. These details are taken directly from the map, but in attempting to measure the actual distance of each day's walk I have made the nearest estimation I could. (With countless zig-zags it is almost impossible to be exact.) Likewise, times are also approximate only and make no allowances for rest stops or photographic interruptions. Inevitably these times will be found slow by some walkers, fast by others. By comparing your times with those given here (and quoted on signposts along the route) you will soon have an idea of how much we differ and adjustments can be made in planning your next day's walk. But remember, this walk is designed for maximum enjoyment of the mountain world and the full experience to be won, it is not intended for racing.

In descriptions of routes, directions 'left' and 'right' apply to the direction of travel, whether in ascent, descent or traverse. However, when used with reference to the banks of glaciers or streams, 'left' and 'right' indicate the direction of flow, ie: looking downwards. Where doubts might occur a compass direction is also given.

Finally I have made every effort to check the route as described for accuracy, and it is to the best of my belief that the guidebook goes into print with all details correct. However, changes do occur from time to time, with paths re-routed and certain landmarks altered. Any corrections to keep the book up-to-date will be made in future printings wherever possible. Should you discover any changes that are necessary (or additions with regard to accommodation, places of refreshment etc.) I would very much appreciate a brief note to that effect. A postcard sent to me via the publisher would be gratefully received.

✻   ✻   ✻

The Alpine Pass Route has already given me more than four of the happiest and most scenic weeks of mountain walking of my career.

If this guidebook encourages you to tackle the route too, and in so doing leads you into realms of beauty and joyful experience, I shall be doubly delighted.

 Accommodation: hotel, gasthof, matratzenlager, mountain hut

 Official campsite

 Refreshments: food or drink

 Funicular, mountain railway

 Cable car

 Gondola lift

 Chair lift

3hrs 45mins Walking time from start of Stage

ROUTE PROFILE KEY

STAGE 1:
SARGANS - MELS - WEISSTANNEN

Distance:	14 kilometres
Time:	3 hours 45 mins.
Start altitude:	482m *High point:* Vermol 1020m
Map:	L.S. 237 Walenstadt 1:50,000
Accommodation:	Sargans - Hotels, gasthofs
	Mels (35 mins) - Hotels, gasthofs
	Weisstannen - Hotel, gasthof
Transport option:	Postbus, (Sargans-Weisstannen)

This first stage is a short and easy one that enables you to break gently into the long walk. It leads away from Sargans and the low, flat valley of the Seeztal, and heads into the lush green Weisstannental to the south-west. As a prelude to the challenge of big mountain country to be experienced later along the Alpine Pass Route, it is ideal for those arriving in Sargans on a midday train; a pleasant afternoon's walk that places you in a good position to tackle the first pass of the route the following day.

Short it may be, but it is not without its moments of steep ascent, and for newcomers to Switzerland this initial stage will open eyes to some of the charms of its villages, its alpine pastures and mountains. The mountains are not high by Alpine standards - those that crowd the head of the valley fail to reach the 3,000 metre mark, and there are no glaciers to speak of - but they are no less attractive for that. The valley itself, the Weisstannental, is green and pastoral with woods clothing the lower hillsides and spilling here and there across the valley floor. At its entrance, behind the village of Mels, the valley is squeezed into a tight defile that only opens with reluctance further south. A road winds in long zig-zags from Mels up the steep guarding slopes and slips into the valley along its eastern side. It's not a busy road for the valley is a dead-end and there will only be light traffic (including Postbuses) making the journey to Weisstannen.

Our route, however, ignores the road initially and climbs out of Mels to enter the valley along its western flanks. It is a fine walk through woods and across open pastures that reaches its high point at the little alp hamlet of Vermol, before easing a way slowly down to river-level at Schwendi, where you either join the road for the walk up to Weisstannen, or take a higher path

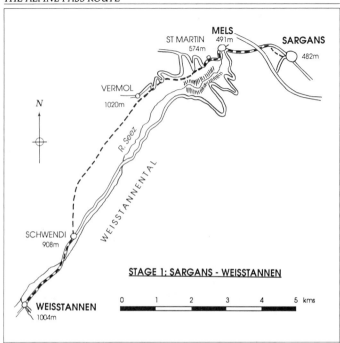

STAGE 1: SARGANS - WEISSTANNEN

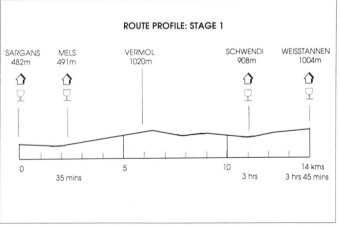

ROUTE PROFILE: STAGE 1

continuing among trees and meadows.

* * *

(1) **SARGANS** (482m) *Hotels, gasthofs, restaurants, shops, PTT, railway station (Zürich-Chur), Postbuses.*

On leaving the Bahnhof (railway station) in Sargans head in a north-westerly direction (ie: towards the town centre) and find a footpath signpost which includes a pointer to Mels and Weisstannen. Continue along the road running parallel with the railway for about 100 metres, where you then cross the road and follow a tarmac path heading along the left-hand side of the Hotel Bahnhof. This path takes you between the railway line and a row of houses, and through gaps between the houses you have views of the town's stately-looking castle and a rather fine church.

At the end of the tarmac path go down some steps to a road and bear left to walk beneath a motorway. Emerging on the western side ignore the *Wanderweg* signpost pointing left, and continue ahead along the road to enter the village of **MELS**. (491m 35 mins *Hotels, gasthofs, shops, PTT, Postbus*)

The heart of Mels is most attractive (the parish church dates from the 9th century), and on coming to the village square with its

Mels

27

fountain, continue to the far side and bear right (there is a sign to Vermol) to cross the River Seez which comes dashing from the tight cleavage of the Weisstannental beyond. A short distance after the bridge cut away sharply to the left up the steeply climbing Burggasse between houses. This brings you onto the road again, having made a short cut, and a moment later you enter the hamlet of **ST MARTIN** (574m) with its beautiful little church seen just ahead.

Stay with the road and walk through St Martin. As soon as you pass through the hamlet you will find yourself above a steep slope of vineyards with good views over the rooftops of Mels to Sargans and the Rhine Valley, with the mountains to the north-east representing tiny Liechtenstein.

Our walk had begun in waterproofs and now, above the vineyards, the rain eased and stopped long enough to allow us to remove cagoules, although clouds hung low over the mountains and promised further showers. Views were restricted, yet there was enough on show to remind us of the splendours of this part of Switzerland - the Churfirsten like wavecrests of rock above the Walensee to the north (unseen from here, but passed a little earlier on the train), the moulding wall of peaks guarding the Rhine's sudden curve northward, and the green slopes that clutched half-hidden alps in a cosy embrace. This was a mere hint of the Switzerland we would be walking through, and despite the clouds with their promise of more rain our enthusiasm for the walk remained undiluted. It was good to be here with rucksacks on our backs and long days of as-yet unknown but suspected enchantment ahead. Our stride was not yet settled, the first steep haul had set us gasping, but we knew it would not be long before a daily pattern of movement and pace would take care of the kilometres and see us tackling each pass with the comfort of fitness.

A few metres beyond the first hairpin bend leave the road on a *Wanderweg* path breaking away to the left and climbing through mixed woodlands. This soon returns you to the road again, but almost immediately take a signposted track (an old road) through the continuing woods. So the route continues; now and again on road, then along signposted woodland tracks.

Still in the woods you come to a junction of tracks at 1,020 metres altitude. (Both tracks are signposted to Weisstannen.) The upper houses of **VERMOL** can just be seen above. Take the left-hand track going downhill a little. This brings you out of the woods to the lower edge of Vermol, continues as a gradual descending traverse of the hillside, and soon becomes a narrow path - once more in woods. This path eventually leads to a string of barns and farms at **SCHWENDI** (908m 3 hours *Gasthof, refreshments, food store*), and onto the main valley road. Head up-valley for about forty minutes, so to reach the pretty little village of **WEISSTANNEN**. (There is an alternative signposted footpath leading from Schwendi which also goes to Weisstannen, but above the road.)

(2) **WEISSTANNEN** (1004m 3 hours 45 mins) *Hotel, gasthof, refreshments, shop, PTT, Postbus.*

*　　*　　*

Places Visited on the Way:
1. **SARGANS:** An ancient small town at the junction of the Seeztal and the Rhine Valley where the latter breaks northward alongside Liechtenstein. Just outside the town to the north the site of a Roman villa was discovered in 1967. Of more recent origin, the old castle (Schloss) that commands the town was built for the former Counts of Toggenburg between the 13th and 15th centuries. (There is a museum in the castle.) Rising above it is the steep little peaklet of Gonzen (1829m), whose ascent is easily made by footpath from Sargans in around 3-3½ hours, and whose summit gives a splendid panorama, including the Walensee and the Rhine Valley from Landquart to the Lake of Constance - but of special interest to APR walkers is the view south-westward into the Weisstannental.

2. **WEISSTANNEN:** This peaceful village is set in an attractive position a little over halfway along its valley, and would make a most pleasant base for a short walking holiday. To the south the enticing valley of the Gufelbach cuts away in a narrow slice. There are high alps to visit and one or two passes to cross, while to the south-west the Weisstannental continues towards its head. A signpost on the edge of the village displays possibilities for a wide variety of walks. As for the village itself, its most attractive feature is the 17th century church dedicated to John the Baptist.

STAGE 2:
WEISSTANNEN - FOOPASS - ELM

Distance:	21 kilometres
Time:	7 hours
Start altitude:	1004m *High point:* Foopass 2223m
Map:	L.S. 247 Sardona 1:50,000
Accommodation:	Elm - Hotel, gasthofs, camping
Transport options:	None

The crossing of the Foopass is a symbolic one, for with over twelve hundred metres of ascent to reach it, and even more to descend from it, it gives a firm idea of the nature of the Alpine Pass Route. With this pass behind you you'll be left in no doubt as to what lies ahead in the days to come.

The day begins easily enough with about 9 kilometres of walking along the valley track-cum-road to its end by the farm at Untersass. There are footpath alternatives available, although these will add a little to the overall distance to be walked, and it is probably better to conserve your energy for the climb to the pass.

At Untersass the climb begins. Although steep in places the path is well-made and clear as far as Fooalp (also known as Alpstafel). From here the way continues without difficulty and meanders over high pastures before tackling the final ascent to the pass. On the western side the initial descent is steep, but soon eases for a pleasant downhill walk into Elm.

✳   ✳   ✳

Leaving Weisstannen continue along the road heading up-valley. This upper part of the Weisstannental is heavily wooded, opening here and there to pastureland, the mountains closing ahead in a neat amphitheatre, streams draining the hillsides into the main valley river, the Seez, which flows parallel to the road. Two kilometres from the village where the road swings right to cross the river, a path continues along the left-hand side (true right bank) and rejoins the road near the farm of **VORSIEZ** (1175m 55 mins) where it recrosses the river once more. There is another footpath alternative which leaves the road just short of Vorsiez, following a track at first, and this rejoins the road at the farm shown as Glätti on the map, but this route is not recommended as it gains too much unnecessary height and later becomes confused in some boggy ground. Better to remain on the road.

The track/road brings you to a farm at **UNTERSASS** (Walabutz) (1361m). Here red-white-red waymarks lead on a continuing track to the left of the farm and wind southwards, soon ending with a clear path that starts to climb in long loops a little west of south. Before long, among shrubs, lovely views are to be had down into the grassy bowl at the head of the valley through which you've been walking, the Weisstannental stretching away as a long green shaft darkened by thick woods.

Making a steady ascent on a well-graded path, the route is brightened not only by the shrubs on the hillside, but by waterfalls seen cascading ahead. Then the path narrows and climbs very steeply to reach **FOOALP** (1875m 3 hours 15 mins) - a solitary farm and a cattle byre on a brief levelling before the mountain rises steeply again.

It had rained all night and was still raining as we set out for the pass. Then, when we reached Fooalp, we came to snow. There were sorrowful-looking cows knee-deep in a mixture of mire and snow, and the hills ahead were piebald with tufts of wet grass poking through the light snow covering. Prospects for the final climb to the pass were not quite what we'd envisaged at home, yet we were not daunted and our spirits remained high - ever optimistic for a return of summer.

If the mire at Fooalp is too deep to face wading through, pass round the right-hand side of the byre and resume on the path beside the farmhouse. It takes you across the stream which flows behind the building and up to a signpost at a junction of paths. Take the right-hand option, in fact virtually straight ahead. It gains height easily heading south, then swings west, clearly marked all the way.

Wading ankle-deep through the snow that threatened to obliterate all sign of the path, we came upon two chamois hunters perched on a rock and passed a few minutes with them. When they heard that we were walking to Montreux they gently chided our folly, saying the English are crazy to do

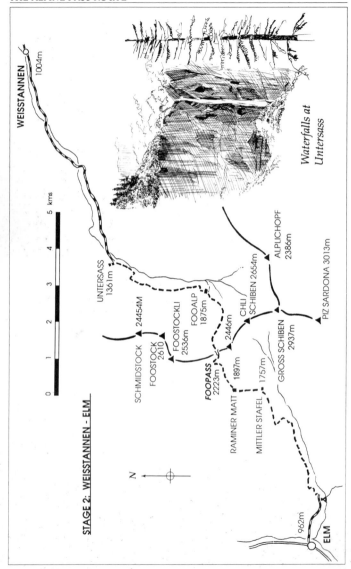

Waterfalls at Untersass

STAGE 2: WEISSTANNEN - ELM

WEISSTANNEN 1004m

5 kms

0   1   2   3   4

N

UNTERSASS 1361m

SCHMIDSTOCK 2445M

FOOSTOCK 2610

FOOSTOCKLI 2536m

FOOALP 1875m

FOOPASS 2223m

2446m

CHLI SCHIBEN 2654m

ALPLICHOPF 2386m

PIZ SARDONA 3013m

GROSS SCHIBEN 2937m

RAMINER MATT 1897m

MITTLER STAFEL 1757m

ELM 962m

32

Urnersee, an indent of the Vierwaldstattersee, seen from Grat - on the way to the Surenenpass (Stage 5)

Blackenalp, on the path from the Surenenpass to Engelberg (Stage 5)

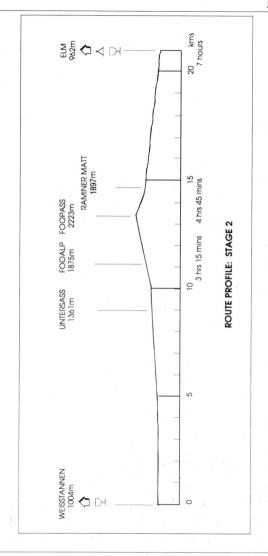

ROUTE PROFILE: STAGE 2

The Wetterhorn above Grindelwald

33

such things. With tongue in cheek I retorted that at least we were moving, and only the Swiss were so crazy as to spend the day frozen on a rock amid the snow waiting for chamois that were bright enough to be down in the forests out of sight of their guns. At one insult each we parted in good humour and headed up towards the heavy clouds.

The path crosses a rough pastureland, over occasional boggy patches, then up a grassy rib of mountainside before easing towards the pass. **FOOPASS** (2223m 4 hours 15 mins) is a slender saddle in the ridge that links the Foostock with Chli-Schiben. From it, in good conditions, views stretch out to include the long ridge of the Hausstock which neighbours the next pass on the itinerary, the Richetli.

On the western side of the pass the path drops steeply at first, then eases to a more gentle descent, clear all the way. About 45 minutes from Foopass you reach the alp of **RAMINER MATT** (also known as Raminer Stafel; 1897m) where the path forks. Take the left branch which soon becomes an easy graded track. Fifteen minutes later you come to a second alp, **MITTLER STAFEL** (1757m 5 hours 15 mins) and turn sharply to the right, with fine views to enjoy. The track grows in size and you swing down through forest, over side streams with occasional views showing across the valley to the slopes of the Tschingelhoren, with more waterfalls in sight, and eventually arrive at a road. Continue down, making long loops with the village of Elm now seen ahead and below, its meadows green and lush, the village appearing attractive and welcoming even from a distance.

As you reach the valley floor you pass an official campsite, but the way continues ahead along the road between meadows, and at last brings you to **ELM**.

(1) **ELM** (962m 7 hours) *Hotel, gasthofs, camping, restaurants, shops, PTT, bus (Elm - Schwanden for rail link with Linthal/Glarus)*

❋   ❋   ❋

Places Visited on the Way:
1. **ELM**: A pretty village, if somewhat strung-out, in a delightful valley. A good opportunity for backpackers to stock-up with food for the onward journey, for among its shops there is a supermarket and a bakery. Its houses are neat and flower-decked; there is a beautiful

church and fine views behind it to Piz Sardona and Piz Segnas. Above the Pass dil Segnas to the east of the village is the so-called St Martin's Hole. Twice yearly (on 12th March and 30th September) at 9.00 am the sun shines through this hole and lights on the tower of Elm church. Up-valley you gaze at the Glarner and Bündner Vorab, and at the Hausstock blocking the valley's end. Trim meadows spread out beyond the village and give no hint of the tragedy which struck on Sunday 11th September 1881 when a steep 500 metre rocky buttress known as the Plattenbergkopf, which for thirteen years had been quarried for slate, suddenly collapsed on the village killing 114 people. (R.L.G. Irving's book *The Alps* - Batsford, 1939 - contains a graphic account of this tragedy.)

The church at Elm

ELM - RICHETLIPASS - LINTHAL

Distance:	20 kilometres
Time:	8 hours
Start altitude:	962m *High point:* Richetlipass 2261m
Maps:	L.S. 247 Sardona & 246 Klausenpass 1:50,000
Accommodation:	Matt (7 hours 50 mins) - Hotel, gasthof
	Linthal - Hotels, gasthof
	Braunwald - Youth Hostel (reached by funicular
	from Matt)
Transport options:	Bus (Elm-Schwanden, thence train to Linthal)

This is the first of several eight-hour days along the Alpine Pass Route, and it is quite a tiring one at that. First comes a valley walk, rising steadily through the lovely pastoral Sernftal with the snows of the Hausstock luring you on. Then, at the head of the valley, the climb begins. A clear path strikes up the hillside in a series of steep sections and finally relents in an upper bowl of meadowland before tackling the last short pull onto the pass.

On the western side begins an equally long and in some respects a tiring descent, rather steep in places but seldom offering any route-finding difficulties. The way down the Durnachtal is more wearying than one might tend to expect, but it is full of interest and being aware that it will require at least an hour and a half to descend once you've actually reached its bed, will go some way towards preparing you for it. Pace yourself for the day, keep your eyes alert to the scenic variety, and you'll have a feast.

Note: *The main route to the pass goes through a military training area at Walenbrugg. On occasion this is temporarily closed to walkers and a sentry will be posted on the road to redirect you. (There is an alternative route available, and this is outlined below.) To check on the situation in advance you may telephone: Zeughaus Glarus, Koordinationsstelle 6 - the number is 058 61 5757. Or call: Truppenlager Matt 058 86 1858.*

✳   ✳   ✳

Stretching beyond Elm the Sernftal is neat and shorn. Meadows step down from the higher crags in a series of natural terraces, crusted with patches of forest here and there, haybarns and individual farms

*Hanenstock and the Kärpf ridge seen from the track
leading away from Walenbrugg*

dotted about the pastures, streams dashing from steep gullies and
shadowed ravines. This is the landscape through which the morning's walk begins, and it is one to enjoy to the full.

Leave Elm heading south-west up-valley. Near the edge of the
village the road forks. Continue ahead and almost immediately
break away left on a signposted footpath (direction Richetlipass). A
fine track takes you along the left-hand side of the river, wandering
through lush green meadows and gradually rising above the Sernft
that seems to be burrowing ever-deeper in its bed. After a short
distance a footpath alternative branches off to the right and edges
round meadows above the river, then takes you back to the main
track again. It is a delightful section of valley to wander through, but

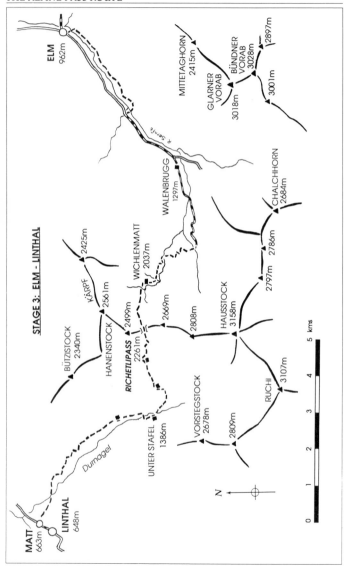

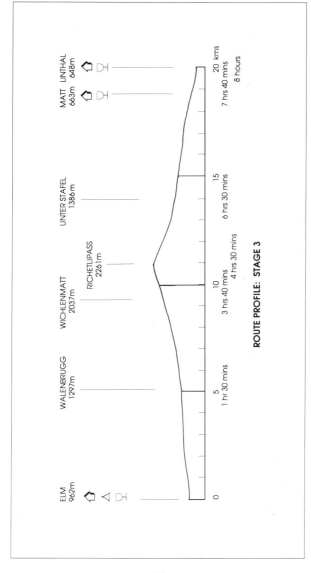

ROUTE PROFILE: STAGE 3

all too soon the track divides and you head to the right, cross the river and follow a footpath steeply up through another meadow to reach the valley road. Here you turn left and continue up-valley.

The military establishment referred to above is situated near the head of the valley at Walenbrugg and the road is often busy with army vehicles trundling to and fro. About 1 hour 15 minutes after leaving Elm you come to a road fork at 1261 metres. A signpost here gives two directions to the Richetlipass. Straight ahead (continuing along the road to Walenbrugg) the route will take 3 hours 15 minutes to the pass; by taking the right-hand option the pass is 3 hours 30 minutes away.

Alternative Route:
By taking the right-hand track you gain height steadily in a series of long loops up the hillside to reach an alp at 1695m (Matt). From here a path continues, climbing more steeply now to pass through a saddle between the rocky Erbser Stock (2182m) and the southern ridge of Karpf. A short descent from this saddle takes you to the alp of Wichlenmatt to join the main route described below.

Main APR:
Continue along the road beyond the fork for a further ten minutes (unless barred by sentries) until shortly before reaching a bridge. Now head off to the right along a clear military road that leads directly to a cattle byre and the military canteen of **WALENBRUGG** (1297m 1 hour 30 mins). Beyond these the road becomes a track heading through rough pastures with lovely views ahead.

Morning at last had dawned bright, and many of the mountains around us were dusted with new snow. By the time we reached Walenbrugg we had warmed to the day and become captured by the views. But just beyond the military canteen our way was barred by an electric fence/barrier. Beyond it the pastures were thick with conscript soldiers attempting to find protection behind low boulders and small hillocks of grass. Clearly an exercise was either in progress, or about to begin. We waited, uncertain whether to turn round or not. There were no sentries to ask. Then along came an army lorry and as I moved the electric fence for it to pass through, asked the driver how

*High above Walenbrugg the route to the Richetlipass
gives some spectacular views*

long we should wait. With a bored lack of concern he told me we could walk on. So we did, nervously expecting at any moment for a blast on a whistle to be a signal for the countryside to erupt with explosions, flying missiles and the whine of bullets. But nothing happened, and the cattle grazing higher in the valley continued to ring their bells to the clear morning air without disturbance.

The track leads to a large basin of grassland at the head of the valley with the fine-looking Hausstock (3158m) towering above. Then it swings to the right and aims up the northern slopes. Where the track finishes a footpath leads on. *(In 1989 work was in progress to extend this track and it is not certain where it is leading. However, Swiss efficiency is certain to ensure that direction signs will be placed at strategic points to keep walkers on the correct route in future.)*

The path climbs steeply, at first with a direct view towards a splendid cascade pouring down the hillside, and beyond to the peaks

Late-summer snow conditions on the Richetlipass

bordering the valley off towards Elm. Then it steepens as it approaches a false col at 1895 metres, crosses a grass-covered crest, goes
over a stream and then enters a beautiful hidden landscape - a great

green bowl of grassland with streams meandering through and the Richetlipass now seen above to the left. It looks suddenly very close.

On coming to the farm building at **WICHLENMATT** (2037m 3 hours 40 mins) the path is joined by another coming from the right. This is the alternative approach route as outlined above.

Bear left, cross the stream and wander ahead over an easy patch of pasture waymarked with paint splashes on rocks. Then the path begins to climb again in a series of zig-zags towards the pass. The slopes leading to it could well be snow-covered at any time of the year, and the path lost beneath it. If this is the case simply kick your way up at the best angle you can find - but beware of cornices on the pass itself.

RICHETLIPASS (2261m 4 hours 30 mins) is a narrow one and a pleasure to reach. Given the right weather conditions views from here are very fine; a maze of ridges and hinted valleys to draw you on.

The descent is very steep on a narrow twisting path that could be rather slippery after rain or melting snow. Lower down its quality improves and you come to a small hut on a hillside spur. Pass this to your left and continue on the path as it drops to a moraine crest. A lovely walk it is along the crest, and at the end you skirt the final cone along its right-hand side and descend to a second small hut. From here the way goes down steeply beside rough crags and among a clutter of wild raspberries to the valley bed of the Durnachtal. Bear right and follow the continuing trail to a bridge which takes you over to the left bank of the Durnagel stream to **UNTER STAFEL** (1386m 6 hours 30 mins).

Just beyond the farm a track takes you over another bridge and back to the right bank. The route now follows this broad track steadily downvalley, passing one or two more farms on the way until it reaches a farm hoist where the track finishes. A footpath continues. (A curious irony in this valley; there is a good quality farm track in its upper reaches and a surfaced road at the bottom, but nothing but a narrow path in the middle! If it were not for the mechanical hoist the upper farms would be very isolated indeed.)

The path leading down sometimes comes upon a one-time mule-trail. More often than not it is steep and narrow as it fights a way

Below the Richetlipass

through thick forest. At one point you are led through a tunnel in the rocks.

At last the route comes upon a minor road which leads directly to the village of **MATT** (663m 7 hours 50 mins; *Hotel, gasthof, refreshments, funicular to Braunwald for Youth Hostel accommodation*) virtually a twin of **LINTHAL**, a short distance down the road to the left.

(1) **LINTHAL** (648m 8 hours) *Hotels, gasthof, restaurants, shops, PTT, Postbus, Railway (Glarus/Zürich)*

* * *

Places Visited on the Way:
1. **LINTHAL:** Together with neighbouring Matt, Linthal does not have the neat compact qualities of some other villages along the route, but it is a pleasant enough place to spend a night in. As with Elm there are opportunities here to stock up with food for the onward journey from a supermarket passed on the road which links the two communities. As for the mountains towering around, pride of place must go to the snow-gemmed Tödi (3614m) at the head of the valley.

44

LINTHAL - KLAUSENPASS - ALTDORF

Distance:	32 kilometres	
Time:	10 hours	
Start altitude:	648m	*High point:* Klausenpass 1948m
Map:	L.S. 246	Klausenpass 1:50,000
Accommodation:	Urnerboden (2hours 30mins) - Hotel, matratzenlager,	
	Unterschächen (7 hours) - Hotel, gasthof	
	Altdorf - Hotels, gasthofs	
	Flüelen - Camping (bus ride beyond Altdorf)	
Transport options:	Postbus (Linthal - Altdorf)	

This very long stage enjoys some splendid views, but in places it entails rather a lot of road walking which can upset the day's pleasures. There are other options available, and one of these is offered below as Alternative Stage 4 which gives a little more than half a day's walking to Urnerboden, thereby giving the opportunity to break the journey to Altdorf into two stages. If this alternative is adopted it will mean, however, that the complete APR will require an additional day to complete.

Another option worth considering is partial use of Postbus in order to avoid the worst of the road work, yet still leaving a very fine day's walking. Only the purist will shun such a suggestion, while those intent on the full enjoyment of the APR as a holiday will find that a judicious use of the Postbus will not detract from the day's enjoyment, but instead may well enhance it. Specific details are given in the main part of the text below.

Given the above comments, this stage is a scenic delight. First there are views to the Tödi to enjoy. Once having climbed out of the Linth valley the valley of Urner Boden is one of the most memorable of all the eastern sections of the Alpine Pass Route. Although a motorist's crossing, the Klausenpass is attractive and certainly less busy than many other Alpine road passes, while the way down from it leads into a magical little village with an easy valley walk beyond it to Unterschächen.

To summarise, prospects of an enjoyable day's walking are limited only by the considerable amount of time required to reach Altdorf, and by the necessity to travel some of the way upon public roads. Both these prospective

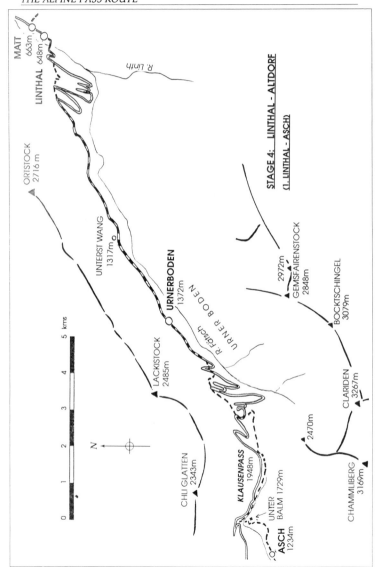

STAGE 4: LINTHAL - ALTDORE
(1. LINTHAL - ASCH)

MATT 663m
LINTHAL 648m
R. Linth
ORISTOCK 2716 m
UNTERST WANG 1317m
URNERBODEN 1372m
R. Fätsch
URNER BODEN
GEMSFAIRENSTOCK 2972m 2848m
BOCKTSCHINGEL 3079m
LACKISTOCK 2485m
CLARIDEN 3267m
2470m
CHLI GLATTEN 2343m
KLAUSENPASS 1948m
UNTER BALM 1729m
ASCH 1234m
CHAMMLIBERG 3169m

N

5 kms
0 1 2 3 4 5

46

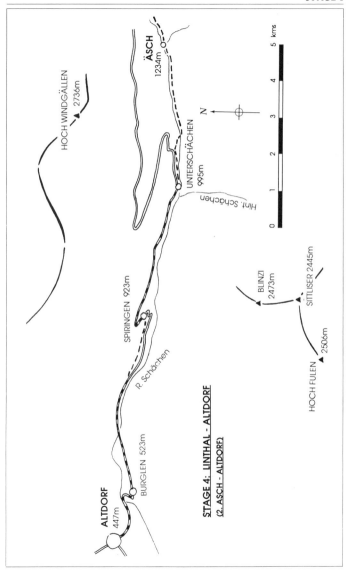

HOCH WINDGÄLLEN 2736m

ÄSCH 1234m

N

UNTERSCHÄCHEN 995m

Hint. Schächen

SPIRINGEN 923m

R. Schächen

BLINZI 2473m

SITTLISER 2445m

HOCH FULEN 2506m

ALTDORF 447m

BURGLEN 523m

STAGE 4: LINTHAL - ALTDORF
(2. ASCH - ALTDORF)

0   1   2   3   4   5 kms

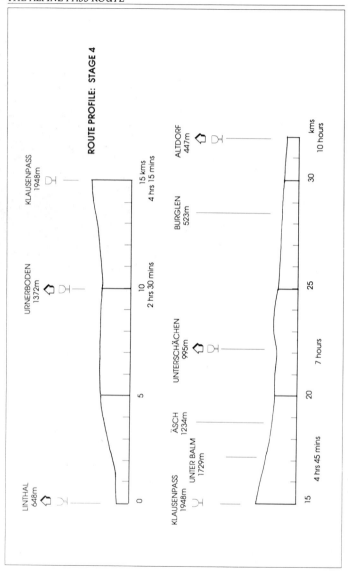

ROUTE PROFILE: STAGE 4

The valley of Urner Boden is one of the finest on the whole walk.
It is seen here about an hour's walk from the Klausenpass

deterrents are easily resolved by use of the Postbus, thereby leaving some delightful country to wander through at leisure.

✳   ✳   ✳

Walk out of Linthal following the Klausen road. Shortly after rounding the first hairpin bend look for a narrow footpath breaking away to the right next to a small stream. There is neither signpost nor waymark to indicate the start of the path, but it is clear enough. It climbs very steeply through lovely mixed woods (walk quietly and you may be rewarded by the sight of chamois) on what was probably an old mule-trail - quite possibly the original route from the Linth valley to that of Urner Boden. When the path emerges from the woods to cross a small open pasture, Tödi is seen shining her snows at the head of the valley.

When you come onto the road cross directly ahead to take the next short stretch of footpath to the road once more. Again you cross

49

The small village of Urnerboden overlooks the valley of the same name.
The mountain at the head of the valley is Clariden (3267m)

directly ahead on the continuing path through yet more woods, eventually coming onto the Klausen road for the last time at a hairpin bend (1117m) where a panorama board highlights the mountains in view.

It will be about 1 hour 30 minutes of road walking from here to the next opportunity to take to footpath again south-west of Urnerboden, and whilst a good part of this is among beautiful mountain scenery, it might be deemed suitable to take a Postbus for at least part of it. If so you will find a Postbus stop a few paces downhill of the hairpin bend. (There is a timetable fixed to it, so you can check when the next bus is due.) **Note:** Do not buy a ticket to take you beyond Urnerboden, though, as some really fine walking is to be had from that little village to the pass.

As you enter the (1) Urner Boden Valley so its visual splendour is laid out for inspection. The right-hand (northern) wall of peaks is almost Dolomitic in scale and stature while those to the south are more gentle and less intimidating. But at the head of the valley the glaciers and small snowfields of Clariden add a certain enchantment to the scene, while the valley itself is luxuriantly rich and green and flat-bottomed, with numerous cows grazing and scatterings of hay barns and farms adding a human scale. As you wander through the valley you pass out of the canton of Glarus and into that of Uri. The Klausenpass is seen ahead. It looks a long way off.

URNERBODEN (1372m 2 hours 30 mins *Hotel, matratzenlager, refreshments, Postbus*) makes a pretty picture with its little church on a bluff with the snow-coated Clariden behind. It's basically a farming community, but would make an idyllic temporary base for a walking holiday as there are many possibilities for interesting tours to be made from here.

Continue along the road for a further 1500 metres or so, then just after rounding the first hairpin bend red and white paint flashes direct you up the grassy bank to the left as a short cut to the next level of road. As you continue towards the pass various other short-cuts are waymarked from the road, and they are all worth taking for they help to gain height and make pleasant walking. Some sections are a little steep, but after yesterday's crossing of the Richetlipass you'll take these in your stride.

One particularly long open hillside stretch gives good views down-valley and brings you onto the road once more at another hairpin bend marked as **VORFRUTT** (1779m) on the map. Here you should turn left and walk downhill a few metres, cross a stream and take a signposted track on the right. This climbs in easy zig-zags to high pastures well away from the road - a lovely patch of country and leads directly to the **KLAUSENPASS** (1948m 4 hours 15 mins *Refreshments, Postbus*).

Whilst you will no doubt regret the coachloads of tourists here, be thankful that at least you will be able to take advantage of the refreshments on offer - one of only three passes on the whole route where this is possible.

The descent begins just beyond the public toilets. There is a signpost indicating the path to Unter Balm and Äsch. The path is rather marshy at first and it runs in a slightly descending traverse a little below the road. There are no waymarks and at times the path is

51

Farmhouse in Äsch,, with a magnificent waterfall behind

unclear, although if you should lose it, simply maintain height and you will come to the road eventually. The path does, in fact, lead to the road where another signpost directs you to backtrack a short distance across a stream, then you veer right (south-east) on the path to Äsch.

It is a grassy path and it takes you again over a stream and in front of the farm buildings of **UNTER BALM** (1729m 4 hours 45 mins). Pass these to your left and locate a waymarked continuing path which swings through a gap and down to pass below a line of cliffs, descending in steep zig-zags with wooden handrails for safety. It's an amazing descent, especially in the mist with the path disappearing into a void below, with little to indicate just how far it will lead.

After the handrails have finished, and near the bottom of the zig-zags, remain alert for an insignificant looking path branching below to the right. There are no signs, waymarks or other indications that this is the path to Äsch, but it is important not to miss it.

Follow this path, sometimes quite steeply, with the Schächental stretching off all green and enticing below, and the village of Äsch soon coming into view. Off to the right a stream comes cascading down a long cleft of hillside; there are pine trees and alpenroses around, and every excuse to dawdle and enjoy the descent to the full.

ÄSCH (1234m 5 hours 30 mins) is idyllic. Its charm lies in its simplicity and its situation, for this clutch of farm buildings is huddled on a rough patch of pastureland below a magnificent water spout. A second part of the hamlet sits on the western side of the river which comes from the waterfall, and consists of flower-bright, worka-day chalets and a tiny church. The whole setting is quite beautiful and certainly justifies the walk to find it.

Continue down-valley on a clear track which is now signposted to Unterschächen; down through pastures and into woods, the river running parallel to the track off to the right, the valley growing a little less trim, but still lovely. Then the track brings you onto the Klausen road once more at **RIBI**, but then you break away on a side path leading off to the left which takes you past more farms and through pastures to the village climbing centre of **UNTERSCHÄCHEN** (995m 7 hours *Hotel, gasthof, refreshments, shops, PTT, Postbus*).

Note: From here to Altdorf involves almost unrelenting road walk-ing, and it may well be worth considering travelling this last long stretch by Postbus.

For those determined to walk, however, no detailed descriptions are necessary. Simply remain on the road virtually all the way to Altdorf. It climbs at first, then runs along the contours before starting to descend to **SPIRINGEN**. There is one possibility of leaving it be-tween Spiringen and Witerschwanden, but otherwise there is little respite from traffic fumes and tarmac under foot. One of the most interesting of villages en route is (2) **BURGLEN** (523m), the last before dropping into **ALTDORF** itself.

(3) **ALTDORF** (447m 10 hours) *Hotels, gasthofs, restaurants, shops, banks, PTT, Postbus, railway (Zürich/Gotthard). Nearest camping at Flüelen (4 kms north by Postbus).*

Note: For those prepared to use public transport, it might be worth considering moving on to Attinghausen in readiness for tomorrow's crossing of the Surenen Pass. Cheaper accommodation is likely to be found there than in Altdorf. (Gasthof Krone [*bedrooms and matratzen-*

lager] is found about 200 metres from the start of the Surenen path.) The Attinghausen bus (not a Postbus) is caught in Altdorf's main square by the Tell statue, or alternatively by the Bahnhof.

The statue of William Tell in Altdorf is reputed to stand on the site of the tree to which his son was tied, when Tell had to shoot the apple from the boy's head

Places Visited on the Way:

1. **URNER BODEN:** This lovely high valley is one of the finest in all Switzerland. It is a long, flat-bottomed pastureland with splendid walls rising on either side. Parts of the valley are a little marshy, but the rich grasslands elsewhere provide summer grazing for something like a thousand cattle. The canton boundary between Glarus and Uri crosses the valley at its north-eastern end.

2. **BURGLEN:** It was here that William Tell was supposedly born and the 16th century chapel, built on what was thought to be the site of Tell's house, was decorated with paintings illustrating his life. There are good views to be had overlooking Altdorf's valley and across to the mountains above Attinghausen where tomorrow's route leads.

3. **ALTDORF:** Capital of canton Uri, Altdorf is inescapably 'Tell's town' with a large bronze statue by Kissling (dated 1895) of the hero standing in the main square (the Rathausplatz) on the site of the tree to which his son was reputedly tied when he had to shoot the apple from his head. It's a busy little town, heavily tourist-orientated, and with plenty of opportunities to change money, buy maps or restock with food.

ALTERNATIVE STAGE 4:
LINTHAL - BRAUNWALD - URNERBODEN

Distance:	13 kilometres
Time:	4 hours 50 mins
Start altitude:	648m *High point:* Usser Alp 1517m
Map:	L.S. 246 Klausenpass 1:50,000,
Accommodation:	Braunwald - Youth hostel, Hotels, Gasthof
	Urnerboden - Hotel, matratzenlager
Transport options:	Funicular (Matt - Braunwald)
	Postbus (Unterst Wang - Urnerboden)

This is one of those balcony walks for which Switzerland is noted. (There will be others along the APR, for example from Engstlenalp to Meiringen [Stage 6], and from Col des Anderéts to Col des Mosses [Stage 14].) It wanders along an upper shelf of hillside at first way above the Linth valley, then veers round to the south-west above the Urner Boden. Views initially are to the Tödi; later to the Clariden and Gemsfairenstock.

Should you choose this option to Stage 4 already described, it would be possible to continue as far as Unterschächen (as per Stage 4 - another 3 hours 30 mins away) and then take Postbus to Altdorf, rather than over night at Urnerboden and continue the walk from here next day. But this would make another long eight-hour day. Better to enjoy this walk at a leisurely pace, and then tackle the onward route to Altdorf tomorrow.

From Linthal station head towards the Braunwald funicular and take the steeply climbing zig-zag path through forest and onto the terrace of hillside where sprawls **BRAUNWALD** (1256m 1 hour 40 mins *Hotels, gasthof, Youth Hostel, refreshments*), a popular traffic-free resort in a sunny position with splendid views to the Tödi. From the funicular station here bear left along a road towards Unter Stafel, then over the Brummbach heading roughly southwards to reach the alp of **RIETBERG** (1362m 2 hours 30 mins). (Magnificent views.)

Take the lower of two paths heading south-west along the upper edge of forest, gaining height at first then descending to **VORDER**

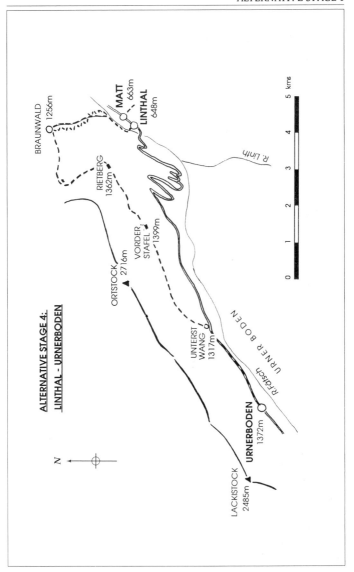

ALTERNATIVE STAGE 4:
LINTHAL - URNERBODEN

BRAUNWALD ○ 1256m

MATT 663m
LINTHAL ○ 648m

R. Linth

RIETBERG ■ 1362m

VORDER STAFEL ● 1399m

ORTSTOCK ▲ 2716m

UNTERST WANG ○ 1317m

Rüchisen

URNER BODEN

URNERBODEN ○ 1372m

LACKISTOCK ▲ 2485m

N

0   1   2   3   4   5 kms

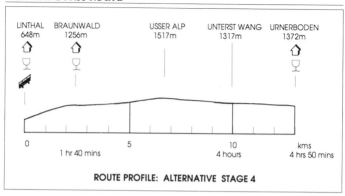

LINTHAL 648m   BRAUNWALD 1256m   USSER ALP 1517m   UNTERST WANG 1317m   URNERBODEN 1372m

0   5   10   kms
1 hr 40 mins   4 hours   4 hrs 50 mins

ROUTE PROFILE: ALTERNATIVE STAGE 4

STAFEL (1399m 3 hours 30 mins). The way continues with the valley of Urner Boden now stretching ahead in a long green shaft, and you come down into its bed at **UNTERST WANG** (1317m 4 hours) and walk alongside the road for another 50 minutes to reach **URNER-BODEN** (1372m 4 hours 50 mins *Hotel, matratzenlager, refreshments, Postbus*).

For route descriptions of the stage **URNERBODEN - ALTDORF** see Stage 4 above.

STAGE 5:
ALTDORF - SURENENPASS - ENGELBERG

Distance:	28 kilometres
Time:	10 hours 15 mins
Start altitude:	447m *High point:* Surenenpass 2291m
Maps:	L.S. 246 Klausenpass & 245 Stans 1:50,000
Accommodation:	Attinghausen (30 mins) - Hotel, gasthof (with matratzenlager)
	Brüsti (3 hours 30 mins) - Gasthof (with matratzenlager)
	Blackenalp (7 hours) - Matratzenlager
	Stäfeli (8 hours) - Matratzenlager
	Alpenrösli (8 hours 30 mins) - Matratzenlager
	Engelberg - Hotels, gasthofs, Youth Hostel, camping
Transport options:	Bus (Altdorf - Attinghausen)
	Cable-car (Attinghausen - Brüsti)

Although this is another exceptionally long day, it is also one of the finest of the whole Alpine Pass Route. Views are glorious nearly every step of the way. The route is clearly defined and, given good weather, it will be a stage to remember and to dream about for years to come.

Once again I am tempted to advise all but the most determined of mountain walkers to take advantage of the transport options available. By so doing you will reduce the day's demands by three hours, which will take away the pressure of time and give you the opportunity to enjoy the route to its fullest. This is, after all, a stage to absorb in every detail, and if there is a section of it which can be ignored, it is the road walk from Altdorf to Attinghausen and subsequent steep, mostly forested uphill path to Brüsti. These can be relieved by taking the local bus from Altdorf to Attinghausen, and the cable-car from there.

From Brüsti, where the cable-car discharges, the approach to the pass is full of variety, with views down to the Vierwaldstattersee or south into the Waldnacht valley. The last part of the ascent takes you over screes, but the way is not difficult and the Surenenpass rewards all who get there with a stunning view south-westward to the Titlis.

The descent is every bit as interesting and scenically spectacular as the

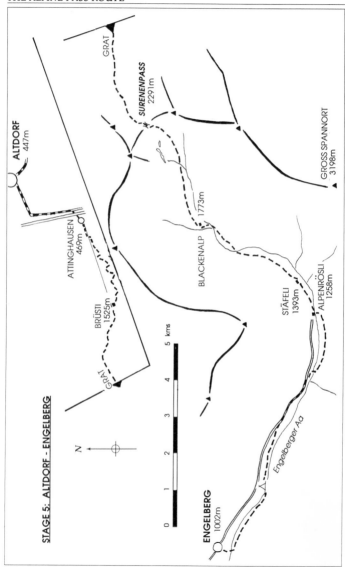

STAGE 5: ALTDORF - ENGELBERG

ALTDORF 447m

ATTINGHAUSEN 469m

BRÜSTI 1525m

GRAT

GRAT

SURENENPASS 2291m

GROSS SPANNORT 3198m

BLACKENALP 1773m

STÄFELI 1393m

ALPENRÖSLI 1258m

ENGELBERG 1002m

Engelberger Aa

N

0 1 2 3 4 5 kms

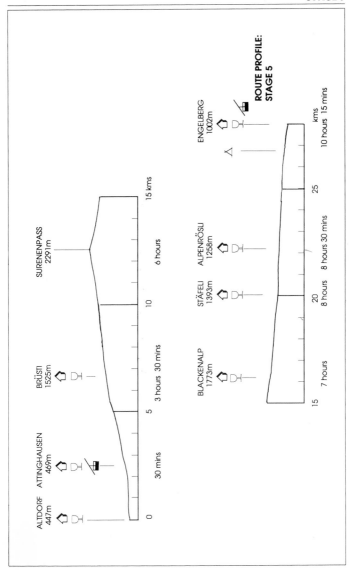

**ROUTE PROFILE:
STAGE 5**

ALTDORF 447m

ATTINGHAUSEN 469m

BRÜSTI 1525m

SURENENPASS 2291m

ENGELBERG 1002m

BLACKENALP 1773m

STÄFELI 1393m

ALPENRÖSLI 1258m

0   30 mins   5   3 hours 30 mins   10   6 hours   15 kms

15   7 hours   20   8 hours   8 hours 30 mins   25   kms   10 hours 15 mins

61

ascent, and it follows a comfortingly graded path all the way down to Engelberg.

On this route there will be several opportunities to rest at wayside farm/ restaurants for a drink, or perhaps to stay overnight at a romantically situated alp with matratzenlager accommodation. Backpackers will be pleased to know that Engelberg's campsite is found on the Surenen side of town and has some of the best facilities of any campsite in Switzerland, including laundry and drying rooms, indoor swimming pool and a well-stocked shop on the site.

❈   ❈   ❈

The walker's route from Altdorf to Attinghausen is best found starting from the town's railway station. This is situated at the south-western edge of town and is approached by a road leading from the Post Office. From the Bahnhof bear left and walk along the street which lies parallel with the railway line, go under the railway, then a motorway, cross the River Reuss and wander uphill into (1) **ATTINGHAUSEN** (469m 30 mins *Hotel, gasthof, shops, bus, cable-car*).

Note: As outlined at the end of Stage 4 details, the Altdorf-Atting-hausen bus stops by the Tell statue in the centre of town. Ask for Attinghausen Seilbahn.

The path to the Surenenpass begins by the side of the cable-car station near a supermarket. (This opens at 7.30 a.m. and is thereby convenient for those staying overnight in the village to buy food for the day prior to setting out for the pass.) A path now leads up along the right-hand side of a stream, rising steadily to the intermediate cable-car station where it crosses the stream and resumes uphill, now more steeply. It is a taxing ascent, soon exchanging pasture for forest, and it climbs in tight zig-zags for over nine hundred metres to **WALDNACHTER** (1402m) where the way divides. Head up to the right on the continuing path to **BRÜSTI** (1525m 3 hours 30 mins *Gasthof with matratzenlager, refreshments*) where the cable-car dis-charges.

Note: Those planning to take the cable-car to Brüsti should bear in mind that the Attinghausen valley station is unmanned and payment is made at the middle station. Passengers must announce their intention to ride by use of an intercom at the bottom station. In the small building you will see a yellow signal button on the wall as you enter. Press this and wait for the engineer's voice to answer. Speak into the microphone grill and announce your wish to ride the cable-car. (*"Bergfahrt, bitte."*) Enter the cable-car and close the door. When ready press another yellow button inside the cabin. This is the signal for the engineer to set the cable-car in motion. Pay at the middle station.

Outside the cable-car station at Brüsti a signpost indicates the uphill path to the Surenenpass. It leads past a few houses and along a short vegetated crest bright with alpenroses, bilberries and stunted pine trees. A short rail-guarded stretch descends slightly alongside a rocky section which gives interesting views down into a scoop of pasture with a few farms and huts dotted about, and across Altdorf's valley to a jumble of mountains running far off. After this you climb up to a splendid green ridge, **GRAT**, which suddenly gives a wonderful sighting of the Urnersee (a leg of the historically important Vierwaldstattersee) way below and to the north, while ahead rises a steep ridge of grey slabs.

The first time I walked this route views were clear and unhindered off to the lake and far away into the contortions of Switzerland's eastern ranges, while wisps of mist played among the grey crags above. But the next time all this was reversed, and a huge cloud-sea hid all sign of lake or valley while the ridges of the Brunnistock were sharp in the morning light, their crests outlined with brush-strokes of cornice. Both times were full of magic and on both occasions I wandered with my heart soaring with the buzzards.

Beyond the green ridge of Grat you will come to **NUSSFRUTTLI** (1953m 5 hours 15 mins), a saddle with the pass seen clearly ahead. The path forks here. The right branch leads in a steady traversing ascent across a scree slope, while the other, waymarked, path descends into a bowl, then climbs more directly to the pass. The upper route is shorter, but in 1989 a warning was painted in red letters on a rock to say that this path across the screes was dangerous and the lower path should be taken. On both my crossings I have taken the upper path across the screes and found no hint of danger or difficulty at all, but each walker should make his own decision as to which

The lake of Seewen, with Titlis in background

route to take. They join forces just below the pass.

The **SURENENPASS** (2291m 6 hours) offers a glorious panorama and, weather permitting, is the sort of place where one is tempted to throw off the rucksack and laze in relaxation, soaking in the peace and the views. The snow-gleam of Titlis (3238m) grabs the attention from the south-west, and as it seems so far off the realisation that tomorrow you will cross its shoulder comes as a sobering prospect. Below the pass, caught in the rucks of sheep pasture, are two or three small tarns. Although the path does not stray to them they make a perfect site for a picnic, but before descending gaze back to the east and try to untangle yesterday's route from the maze of peak and valley spread out in the blue distance. It's a bewildering and complex vista, full of charm and mystery.

The continuing path descends easily, swinging down in lazy twists and turns into a contorted landscape roughened aeons ago before the mountains cooled properly. Sheep graze here and there, their high-pitched tinkling bells contrasting with the deeper clang you've become accustomed to from cowbells. It is a clear path and a popular one, and on a summer's day you will no doubt have company along

The Lauterbrunnen valley from above Wengen (Stage 8)

Wetterhorn, Eiger and Mönch from Brünli (Stage 9)

it. After the comparative solitude of Foopass and the Richetli, this meeting with other walkers comes as something of a surprise, but you will become used to it as you wander into the Bernese Oberland, and it will not be until you leave Gsteig, several days hence, that you begin to have the mountains to yourself once more.

An hour from the pass brings you to **BLACKENALP** (1773m 7 hours, *Matratzenlager, refreshments*), a solitary farm in the mouth of a very fine cirque of mountains topped by the Wissigstock (2887m) and Blackenstock (2930m). The farm serves drinks, and has accommodation for thirty. Nearby stands a most attractive little white-walled chapel.

Just beyond the farm the path drops through a little natural gateway, crosses the stream (the Stierenbach) and breaks into an open section of valley, seen stretching far ahead. Always clear and adequately signposted at all junctions, the path makes for easy and enjoyable walking. The views are never less than magnificent, with streams, cascades, big mountains rising all around, hillsides ringing with cowbells, flowers blooming, alpenroses offering darker patches of greenery .... it's everything an Alpine walk should be.

The valley levels and you come to **BERGGASTHAUS STÄFELI** (1393m 8 hours *Matratzenlager, refreshments*). From the terrace tables here eyes are magnetically drawn across the valley to a stab of aiguilles of the Spannorter rising against the skyline; dreaming spires to taunt ambition.

From Stäfeli the path becomes a track, but within a few paces it veers left and a narrow waymarked path continues straight ahead. Follow this path. It takes you among trees for about half an hour and then leads directly to another gasthof, this one **ALPENRÖSLI** (1258m 8 hours 30 mins *Matratzenlager, refreshments*).

Here you cross the river and bear right to follow a narrow path over pastures and through woods. (It is perfectly feasible to follow the broad track from Alpenrösli to the main valley road, but the footpath route is much more enjoyable.) The path maintains a close companionship with the river. Do not be drawn away to the left where another path climbs higher, but remain near the river until at last you are led over it and onto the track. Soon you can desert this by cutting

Grazing cow above Mürren

*On the descent from the Surenenpass the path leads across the
mouth of a fine amphitheatre of mountains at Blackenalp*

straight ahead across pastures where the track swings to the right,
then join the valley road for the final walk down into Engelberg. (A
better option is to take a riverside path which you join on the downstream side of a gravel extraction works, and halfway through
Engelberg's campsite cross to the left bank and follow the *Professorweg* all the way into Engelberg.)

(2) **ENGELBERG** (1002m 10 hours 15 mins) *Hotels, gasthofs, Youth
Hostel, camping, restaurants, shops, banks, PTT, Postbus, railway, cable-
cars.*

✳   ✳   ✳

Places Visited on the Way:
1. **ATTINGHAUSEN:** A village that is very much overshadowed by
its neighbour Altdorf. It was the birthplace of Walter Furst, Baron
Attinghausen who, with two others, was an original conspirator
against Habsburg rule. Schiller's William Tell has Furst as one of its
characters. Attinghausen today appears to be a 'commuter' village,

The Alpine Chapel at Blackenalp

but is well-placed for walkers on the Alpine Pass Route and offers an alternative overnight stop to the busier and more expensive Altdorf.

2. ENGELBERG: The first of the major mountain resorts visited along the route, Engelberg makes a fine walking centre. A number of interesting excursions are made possible from a base here, several aided by a variety of cable-cars and chair-lifts. The town, however, is much older than tourism, for it developed around a Benedictine abbey (founded 1120, but rebuilt after being burnt down a third time, in 1730-37) and named by Pope Calixtus II, *'Mons Angelorum''* - from whose German form is derived the name of Engelberg. It is a town of considerable appeal, and with some delightful views to the head of the valley.

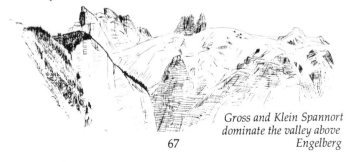

Gross and Klein Spannort dominate the valley above Engelberg

67

STAGE 6:
ENGELBERG - JOCHPASS - MEIRINGEN

Distance:	31 kilometres
Time:	9 hours 30 mins
Start altitude:	1002m *High point:* Jochpass 2207m
Maps:	L.S. 245 Stans & 255 Sustenpass 1:50,000
Accommodation:	Gerschnialp (1 hour) - Pension
	Trübsee(2 hours 30 mins) - Hotel
	Jochpass (3 hours 50 mins) - Gasthof/matratzenlager
	Engstlenalp (4 hours 50 mins) - Hotel
	Reuti (8 hours 15 mins) - Hotels
	Meiringen - Hotels, Youth Hostel
Transport options:	Cable-car (Engelberg - Trübsee)
	Chair-lift (Trübsee - Jochpass)
	Chair-lift (Jochpass - Engstlensee)
	Postbus (Engstlenalp - Meiringen)
	Cable-car (Reuti - Meiringen)

Another long and demanding day, if taken in its entirety on foot, but with plenty of options available to allow this stage to be broken with overnight accommodation at one of several fine places, or with judicious aid of available transport, it becomes a much less daunting section.

It is a scenically delightful route. On the approach to the pass there are soft pastures, forest walks and Titlis soaring overhead. The Trübsee is a charming lake set in a high amphitheatre of peaks, while on the descent to Engstlenalp the gleam of the larger Engstlensee draws you down. The walk to Meiringen is a belvedere, it takes you along a high balcony of a path above the beautiful Gental, with the Wetterhorn growing out of the landscape ahead. Long views, close views, and a rich variety of flowers, make this a stage to enjoy.

For the purist the presence of cable-cars and chair-lifts practically all the way to the pass may seem an intrusion. Indeed, it is difficult to come to terms with them when you recall the glorious semi-wilderness aspect of some of the crossings of the APR, but they do have their uses, and I would suggest for anyone with a tight schedule to maintain that it could be worth taking uplift to the Jochpass. This will allow plenty of time (and energy) to walk all the way to Meiringen and in so doing give the opportunity to enjoy an ancient path

The Trubsee

that links several isolated alps. *An alternative suggestion is to walk to the pass and descend to Engstlenalp, and then continue down into the Gental and catch a Postbus to Meiringen from one of the valley villages when you run out of time or energy.*

✻   ✻   ✻

If setting out from the campsite up-valley of Engelberg, cross the river by way of a footbridge in the middle of the site and head downstream on the left bank along a clear path known as the *Professorweg.* Within a few hundred metres you will come to a signpost directing you up a path on the left which cuts across a short meadow and through forest to **GERSCHNIALP** (otherwise known as **VORDER STAFEL** 1257m 1 hour *accommodation, refreshments*).

If, however, you start from Engelberg proper, follow signposts that take you over the river and up to **GASTHAUS BANKLIALP** where a continuing clear way leads into forest with a steep climb to the open meadowland of **GERSCHNIALP/VORDER STAFEL.**

From here the path takes you towards the steepening slope of mountainside which you climb in an interminable series of zig-zags while brightly painted gondolas swing overhead with effortless ease.

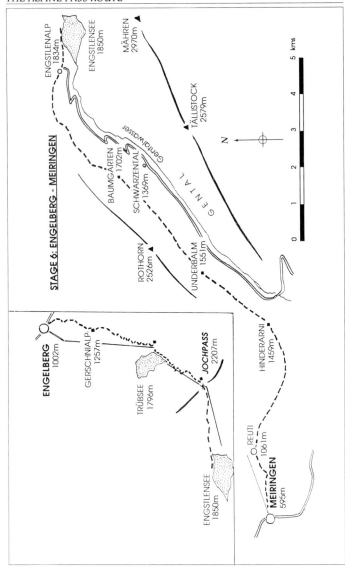

STAGE 6: ENGELBERG - MEIRINGEN

ENGSTLENALP 1834m
ENGSTLENSEE 1850m
MÄHREN 2970m
TÄLLISTOCK 2579m
Gentalwasser
GENTAL
BAUMGÄRTEN 1702m
SCHWARZENTAL 1369m
ROTHORN 2526m
UNDERBALM 1551m
N
5 kms

ENGELBERG 1002m
GERSCHNIALP 1257m
JOCHPASS 2207m
TRÜBSEE 1796m
HINDERARNI 1459m
ENGSTLENSEE 1850m
REUTI 1061m
MEIRINGEN 595m

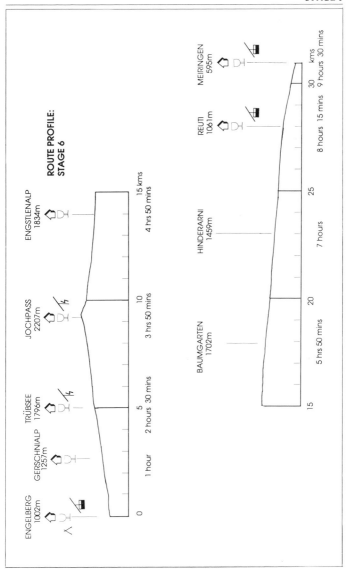

ROUTE PROFILE: STAGE 6

ENGELBERG 1002m

GERSCHNIALP 1257m

TRÜBSEE 1796m

JOCHPASS 2207m

ENGSTLENALP 1834m

BAUMGARTEN 1702m

HINDERARNI 1459m

REUTI 1061m

MEIRINGEN 595m

0   1 hour   2 hours 30 mins   3 hrs 50 mins   4 hrs 50 mins   5 hrs 50 mins   7 hours   8 hours 15 mins   9 hours 30 mins

0   5   10   15   20   25   30 kms

71

The way becomes even steeper towards the top of this section of climb and you emerge onto a sudden levelling by the side of the hotel and gondola lift station above the **TRÜBSEE** (1796m 2 hours 30 mins *accommodation, refreshments*). Join the crowds wandering straight ahead down a broad track into a large, hidden plateau and take the continuing path along the left-hand end of the lake. (There is a remarkable view to the (1) **TITLIS** rising high above you to the left.)

Follow round the edge of the lake towards the chair-lift that goes to the Jochpass. Just before coming to the chair-lift station the path breaks away to the left and begins an hour's climb to the pass. It is not a difficult path, but it is eroded and has the disadvantage of chair-lifts passing overhead almost the entire way. Look out for marmots as you approach the pass.

Reach the **JOCHPASS** (2207m 3 hours 50 mins *accommodation, refreshments*) with its cluster of buildings and mechanical aids, and take the continuing path that heads south-westward beneath yet another chair-lift. Fortunately you soon lose this on the way down towards Engstlensee, the large oval lake seen some 300 metres below. Ahead the Wetterhorn appears like a great meringue-topped cake, and it will remain in sight for several hours yet.

As you reach the **ENGSTLENSEE** (1850m 4 hours 30 mins) pause to enjoy the very fine views back towards the pass. The lake is set within a sweep of pasture, but its southern side rises dramatically to a wall of peaks topped with small glaciers and snowfields, and runs north-eastwards to the Titlis. The lakeside is a popular place with picnic parties and anglers. There is a road which approaches within a few hundred metres and holiday-makers crowd here to enjoy the beauty of the place. And who can blame them?

Continue along the main path which draws away from the lakeside and takes you directly to **ENGSTLENALP** (1834m 4 hours 50 mins *accommodation, refreshments, Postbus*) with its hotel, car park and the beginning of the road that goes down through the Gental to Innertkirchen and Meiringen in the Haslital. At this point you have a choice of routes. The main route described below leads along the north-western side of the valley on the balcony path high above the Gental.

Alternative Route:

The alternative route takes you down into the valley (the path crosses the road near the Engstlenalp hotel and cuts down at first through woods, then over pastures). It is a most enjoyable walk, taking you below a wonderful collection of waterfalls bursting out of the mountain wall, through one pasture after another, but then brings you onto the road at Schwarzental.

Either catch the Postbus here, or continue down the road to Gentalhütten and catch the Postbus to Meiringen from there. To walk all the way to Meiringen by this alternative is rather pointless as it will entail rather too much road walking. It does, however, give backpackers the option of camping at Innertkirchen where the Gental flows into the Haslital. (**Note** that there is no campsite in Meiringen.) There is one additional option to consider, and that is to follow the Gental beyond the hamlet of Gentalhütten to a short distance beyond the small tarn that is found towards the lower end of the valley. A signposted path/track leads away from the road here, on its right-hand side, and takes about 3 hours to reach Meiringen. It passes through Grüebi and, waymarked and signposted, swings round the mountainside on a lower level than the main APR route before dropping into Meiringen.

Main APR:

From the hotel at Engstlenalp take the path heading off to the right, signposted to Hasliberg and Reuti. It takes you past haybarns and farms with lovely views both up and down-valley, then swings westward over a green undulating hillside with streams flowing through and memorable views ahead to the Wetterhorn. The path crosses a stream and begins its belvedere course along the mountainside which you follow for the next three hours. It is a marvellous afternoon's walk. For much of the time the Wetterhorn lures you on. Flowers adorn the pathside. There are views into the Gental below - early on you gaze directly at the waterfalls bursting out of the mountain wall opposite - and the long green trench displays its gentle characteristics to you even from a distance. There are few alps along the way, and no opportunities for refreshment (other than from a mountain stream or water trough) between Engstlenalp and Reuti nearly 3$^{1}/_{2}$ hours apart.

My first jaunt along the APR had led me down into the Gental and I remembered it with great affection - especially the waterfalls and soft pastures. But now, walking the upper path, I was totally absorbed by the beauty of the place. At all times the views were glorious and my camera-finger was soon aching. The sun burned brightly and crickets were brought out of rest to fill the air with their noisy buzzing; it was an afternoon that I was in no hurry to see fade into evening.

At times the path is narrow and a little exposed, sometimes it fades to a mere trail of brushed grass, but mostly it is clear beaten earth and seen far ahead as it climbs and falls over an assortment of undulations. **BAUMGARTEN** (1702m 5 hours 50 mins) is the first alp along the way, a handful of buildings perched on a natural terrace of hillside and with a farm road leading up to it from the valley. The path continues ahead.

At **UNDERBALM** (1551m) a spring-fed pipe gushes into a water trough and gives the opportunity to fill water bottles; at **HINDER-ARNI** (1459m 7 hours) you gaze south over the slope of mountains that stand guard at the entrance to the Gental and up to the big wall of peaks crowding the Grimsel Pass. Here the path curves to the right above the Haslital and joins a broad track. This takes you through patches of forest and out between pastures, always with views to enjoy, and still high above the valley.

The track leads all the way to (2) **REUTI** (1061m 8 hours 15 mins *accommodation, refreshments, cable-car, Postbus*), but there are sign-posted short-cuts that take you down to the village too. It will take at least another hour to walk down to Meiringen, but should you be feeling too weary to face a knee-jarring descent, there are transport options available - either by cable-car or by Postbus.

From Reuti signposts direct the continuing path down to Meirin-gen. It first crosses pastureland on the edge of the village, then ducks into forest where the way is very pleasant but becoming rather steep as it descends a long twisting course, and then at last brings you to the north-eastern edge of town near the cable-car station. It will take only a few minutes of walking to bring you into the heart of **MEIRINGEN**.

(3) **MEIRINGEN** (595m 9 hours 30 mins) *Hotels, Youth Hostel, restaurants, shops, banks, PTT, Postbus, railway (Brienz/Interlaken), cable-car. Nearest camping at Innertkirchen (via Postbus).*

Note: There is matratzenlager accommodation to be had twenty minutes' from Meiringen at Hotel Tourist, Willigen on the route of tomorrow's stage. (See route description under Stage 7 below.)

✳   ✳   ✳

Places Visited or Seen on the Way:

1. **TITLIS:** The Titlis is a grand-looking mountain, despite its lacework of cableways. At 3238 metres it was the first of Switzerland's snow mountains to be climbed. This was achieved in 1744. Nowadays you can take a cable-car to the Klein Titlis (3028m) along the ridge to the west of the main summit, where there is glacier skiing to be had. Views from the summit are extensive and stretch across much of the Alpine chain from the snows of Mont Blanc to the Tyrol. The Black Forest and the ridge of the Jura can also be seen, but it is the big peaks of the Oberland that dominate.

2. **REUTI:** A small village rapidly developing into a sunny resort high above the Haslital. It is linked with Meiringen by cable-car that also extends to Bidmi, and from there to Magisalp. From Magisalp a chair-lift continues to Planplatten (2186m) which makes accessible some very fine walking country. Magisalp and Planplatten are also popular venues for winter skiing.

3. **MEIRINGEN:** This busy little town occupies a fairly level site between the River Aare and the slopes of the Hasliberg, and grew in importance as a result of the increase in traffic using the Brunig, Susten and Grimsel passes. It has a long history, but few of its buildings survived two major fires: the first in 1879, the second in 1891. One which did survive is the lovely 14th century church seen as you enter the town from Reuti. The Reichenbach Falls are among the town's greatest tourist assets, and it was here that Conan Doyle set Sherlock Holmes's confrontation with Professor Moriarty. This connection with the fictional Holmes is today unashamedly exploited in Meiringen's publicity. Another natural feature of great appeal is the Aareschlucht, a spectacular gorge with a walkway through it. This is found a short distance up-valley towards Innertkirchen.

MEIRINGEN - GROSSE SCHEIDEGG - GRINDELWALD

Distance:	21 kilometres
Time:	7 hours 30 mins
Start altitude:	595m *High point:* Grosse Scheidegg 1962m
Map:	L.S. 5004 Berner Oberland 1:50,000
Accommodation:	Willigen (20 mins) - Hotel, matratzenlager
	Schwendi (50 mins) - Gasthof/matratzenlager
	Zwirgi (1 hour 20 mins) - Gasthof
	Kaltenbrunnen (2 hours 15 mins) - Gasthof
	Rosenlaui (3 hours) Hotel
	Schwarzwaldalp (3 hours 35 mins) Gasthof/ matratzenlager
	Grosse Scheidegg (5 hours 20 mins) - Hotel/ matratzenlager
	Grindelwald - Hotels, gasthofs, Youth Hostel, camping
Transport option:	Postbus (Meiringen - Grindelwald via Grosse Scheidegg)

A comparatively easy day's walking, this stage leads into one of the best known of all regions of the Bernese Oberland, passing below the steep walls of the Wetterhorn and providing the first view of the notorious Eiger. A brief glance at the map would suggest that much of this route is along a road. Happily that is not so and there are many variants possible to ensure that you remain on footpaths nearly all the way.

Having left the Haslital you enter the more narrow, wooded Reichenbach valley. Under a heavy sky this valley can seem somewhat gloomy and oppressive, but with sunshine it becomes a delight, opening beyond Gschwantenmad with the towering Wellhorn and the Rosenlaui Glacier suspended just ahead, while the great pinnacled wall of the Engelhörner on the left rightly suggests a rich playground for rock climbers. Here you can either continue along the road (there is little traffic) to Rosenlaui and Schwarzwaldalp, or cut away from it on a pleasant footpath.

From Schwarzwaldalp only Postbuses and vehicles delivering to the hotel at Grosse Scheidegg are permitted to continue up the road, so it makes quite a pleasant walk on its own, but there are paths to take you through lovely pastures and among trees and shrubs as you rise to the pass in the shadow of the Wetterhorn.

Grosse Scheidegg is a busy place, but not as busy as the Kleine Scheidegg seen on the skyline as a saddle below the north face of the Eiger. Grindelwald sprawls below in a broad sweep of meadow, and a variety of paths lead you to it with mountains growing familiar as you descend - familiar even if you've never been there before, for this is a landscape straight out of calendars and chocolate boxes and so many books of mountaineering history.

To leave Meiringen follow the main road heading south (direction Innertkirchen and Grimsel Pass), cross the River Aare and enter the village of **WILLIGEN** (621m 20 mins *accommodation, refreshments, shop*). About 50 metres beyond Hotel Tourist turn right along a narrow road between a house and a barn. Pass several houses and when the road ends continue along a grass path rising quite steeply ahead. This brings you to a narrow road which you follow briefly before cutting away again on the continuing path. The path leapfrogs the road here and there (always signposted or waymarked), over pastures and among woods. At the head of one these pastures you come to the hamlet of **SCHWENDI** (792m 50 mins *accommodation, refreshments, Postbus*).

Continue along a combination of road and footpath, still gaining height in order to enter the Reichenbach valley. After one pleasant forest section you come onto the road once more with the path continuing on the opposite side up a flight of steps and alongside **GASTHAUS ZWIRGI** (983m 1 hour 20 mins *accommodation, refreshments*).

After another footpath section you come to the road and follow it for a while, passing as you do a solitary gasthof/restaurant, **KALTENBRUNNEN** (1210m 2 hours 15 mins *accommodation, refreshments*). By now the gradient has eased and the valley stretches ahead, densely wooded and steep-walled.

It broadens and becomes less forbidding as you approach an open pasture with the Rosenlaui Glacier seen directly ahead, hanging against the side of the grey wall of the Wellhorn (3192m). Views are inspiring. There are the jagged Engelhörner peaks to the left cutting south into a world of ice. Then there's the broken snout of the

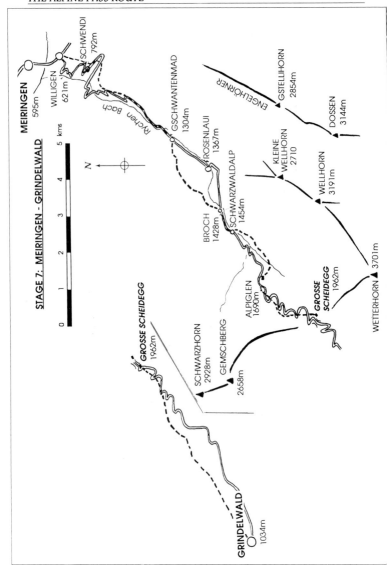

STAGE 7: MEIRINGEN - GRINDELWALD

0 1 2 3 4 5 kms

N

MEIRINGEN 595m
WILLIGEN 621m
SCHWENDI 792m

Rychen Bach

GSCHWANTENMAD 1304m
ROSENLAUI 1367m
BROCH 1428m
SCHWARZWALDALP 1454m
ALPIGLEN 1690m
GROSSE SCHEIDEGG 1962m

ENGELHÖRNER
GSTELLIHORN 2854m
DOSSEN 3144m
KLEINE WELLHORN 2710m
WELLHORN 3191m
WETTERHORN 3701m

GROSSE SCHEIDEGG 1962m
SCHWARZHORN 2928m
GEMSCHBERG 2658m

GRINDELWALD 1034m

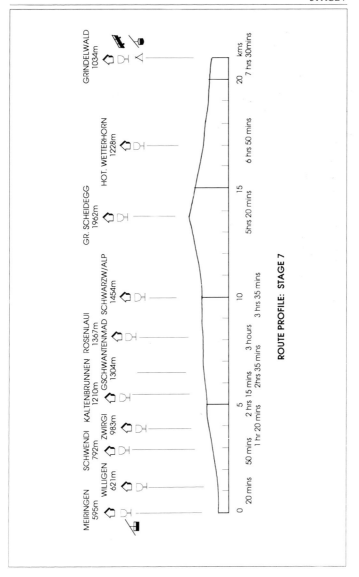

ROUTE PROFILE: STAGE 7

Rosenlaui Glacier, the great slabs of the Wellhorn and, round more to the south-west, the snows of the Wetterhorn. Under a bright sky everything gleams and sparkles and the contrast of dark pine forest below and crystal snow above, makes a splendid picture.

This is **GSCHWANTENMAD** (1304m 2 hours 35 mins), a collection of farms and barns where pigs are often seen wandering across the road - or even sleeping on it! Here you have a choice of routes to take.

Alternative Route:

Continue ahead following the road, which in a little under half an hour brings you to (1) **ROSENLAUI** (1367m 3 hours *accommodation, refreshments*). The road breaks away sharply here to cross the river, and then continues heading up-valley to recross once more by the alp of **BROCH**, where the main route (described below) emerges. A short distance from Broch you come to the end of the public road, so far as motorists are concerned, at **SCHWARZWALDALP**.

Main APR:

Leave the valley road at Gschwantenmad and take the farm road heading to the right across the pasture. A convenient footpath soon leaves this, heads through some trees, over more pasture and rejoins the farm road at the start of an open region of grazing land, **RUFENEN** (1400m), with some superb mountain views. A signpost here directs you away from the farm road across the pastures on the left, in the direction of Broch and Schwarzwaldalp. Wandering through woods you come to a particularly boggy stretch where the crossing is made by a path strengthened by a long succession of logs a veritable boardwalk. The path regains the valley road at the hamlet of farms of **BROCH**. Bear right along the road and in a few minutes you will come to **SCHWARZWALDALP** (1454m 3 hours 35 mins *accommodation, refreshments, Postbus*).

It was a cold, overcast morning and the prospect of a hot drink was too tempting to resist. Leaving our rucksacks against the wall we went inside the gasthof, into a warm room full of climbers and walkers, full of the smell of coffee and cooking, the windows steamed, a babble of voices rising and falling in laughter from a group of climbers whose ropes and rucksacks were piled beside their table. There were large coloured posters on the walls depicting rock climbers in action on the Engelhörner; others showing the Wetterhorn caked in winter snow and looking pristine in February sparkle. Coffee came in large generous bowls, creamy but strong. We ate almond pastries and as the clock ticked off the minutes, found ourselves sliding into the warm comfort of relaxation; the kind of relaxation that makes it difficult to break free. And there was danger then in seeing the day drift aimlessly by. We still had four hours of walking to attend to .... but it was warm and cosy in the restaurant and there was a reluctance to move. That is, until the waitress placed before the climbers great platters of bratwürst and rösti, with side plates of green salad and tomatoes. That was too cruel for us. We paid our bill and scurried outside, heaved the rucksacks onto our shoulders and strode away from temptation.

A few paces beyond Chalet Schwarzwaldalp leave the road and follow a path heading left, signposted to Alpiglen. This is a very pleasant footpath which heads among trees and shrubs (pine, rowan and bilberries) at the foot of the Wellhorn. It eventually crosses the stream and comes to an area of rough pasture and returns you to the road near a farm building. Nearby the continuing path is found on the right-hand side of the road. From here to Grosse Scheidegg simply follow the path which crosses and recrosses the road and at last emerges beside the large hotel at **GROSSE SCHEIDEGG** (1962m 5 hours 20 mins *accommodation, refreshments, Postbus*).

The pass is a true saddle slung between the north-western wall of the (2) Wetterhorn and the insignificant Schwarzhorn. From it you gaze over the rich meadows of Grindelwald to the Männlichen ridge. Tracing that ridge leftwards you can easily make out tomorrow's pass, the Kleine Scheidegg. And rising savagely to the left of that is the Eiger. Turning back to study the way you've come, there is a fine collection of rocky peaks in view stretching in a line above the Reichenbach valley. But high above the pass the snowfields and hanging glaciers of the Wetterhorn are often jettisoning their excesses, and this is a good place to watch the avalanches rolling - especially in early summer.

The way down to Grindelwald is easy and needs little description.

The unmistakable outline of the Wetterhorn
rises dramatically over Grindelwald

There are soon numerous routes to choose from, each one timed so you can take your pick. But first take the path seen cutting directly below the Grosse Scheidegg. It crosses the road several times, going across rough pastures, passing the occasional haybarn - always with superb views to the Oberer Grindelwald Glacier flowing between the Wetterhorn and Mattenberg - and then becomes confused by alternatives. Each one is signposted. Make your choice and enjoy the descent, the views, the chalets with their window boxes bright with petunias and geraniums, and the fragrance of the hay. It will be a little more than two hours from the pass before you reach **GRINDEL-WALD**.

(3) **GRINDELWALD** (1034m 7 hours 30 mins) *Hotels, gasthofs, Youth Hostel, camping, restaurants, shops, banks, PTT, Postbus, railway (Kleine Scheidegg/Jungfraujoch/Interlaken), cable-cars, chair-lifts etc.*

✳   ✳   ✳

Places Visited or Seen on the Way:

1. **ROSENLAUI:** A small collection of buildings backed by trees that passes as a climbing centre and secluded resort. It began life as a spa, but is now better known as home of the Swiss National Mountaineering School. The river here forms an attractive waterfall; nearby to the east is a glacier gorge (Gletscherschlucht) with a popular path climbing through to allow a close view of the Rosenlaui Glacier. Of particular attraction to climbers based here are the various pinnacles of the Engelhörner, the Wellhorn and Wetterhorn.

2. **THE WETTERHORN:** Dominating the valley of Grindelwald this is one of the most celebrated and easily recognised mountains in all the Alps, although it is by no means one of the highest. It has three main peaks: the Rosenhorn (3689m), Mittelhorn (3704m) and the true Wetterhorn, the Hasli Jungfrau (3701m), first climbed in 1844. Alfred Wills' ascent in September 1854, vividly described in his classic *Wanderings in the Alps*, was considered to be the start of the so-called Golden Age of Mountaineering.

3. **GRINDELWALD:** Formerly noted as the 'glacier village' Grindelwald is now one of Switzerland's busiest resorts and mountaineering centres, alive and thriving equally in winter as in summer. Its glaciers

were subjected to considerable scientific interest in the 17th century, and in the early 19th century attracted the attention of inquisitive tourists. The glaciers (Upper and Lower) have since receded a fair distance, but remain a curiosity (if a minor one) to non-mountaineering visitors to this day. Many of today's Grindelwald visitors are, however, attracted to the famous and (highly expensive) Jungfraujoch railway. This leaves Grindelwald Grund station for Kleine Scheidegg and the long tunnel through the Eiger, from which it emerges at the Joch (or saddle) below the Jungfrau at a height of 3454 metres - the highest railway in Europe. Other attractions of Grindelwald include, of course, the exceptional scenery and very fine walking prospects. A walking holiday based here would provide plenty of variety and stimulating exercise for any keen rambler, while for trekkers on the Alpine Pass Route it would make an obvious choice for a brief rest from the long walk. It also provides an opportunity to replenish supplies, films, maps or to replace any equipment damaged along the way.

The edge of a glacier
above Schwarzwaldalp

GRINDELWALD - KLEINE SCHEIDEGG - WENGEN - LAUTERBRUNNEN

Distance:	19 kilometres
Time:	6 hours 30 mins
Start altitude:	1034m *High point:* Kleine Scheidegg 2061m
Map:	L.S. 5004 Berner Oberland 1:50,000
Accommodation:	Alpiglen (2 hours 20 mins) - Hotel/matratzenlager
	Kleine Scheidegg (3 hours 50 mins) -
	Hotels/matratzenlager
	Wengen (5 hours 30 mins) - Hotels
	Lauterbrunnen - Hotels, camping
Transport options:	Train (Grindelwald - Kleine Scheidegg)
	Gondola lift (Grindelwald - Männlichen)
	Train (Kleine Scheidegg - Wengen - Lauterbrunnen)
	Cable-car (Männlichen - Wengen)

This stage will rarely be tackled in solitude. There are crowds in Grindelwald, crowds at Kleine Scheidegg and plenty of people at Wengen too. And in between the footpaths are well trodden, and rightly so. This is a cornerstone of the Alps; the fabled tryptich of Eiger, Mönch and Jungfrau beckoning, and each pathway seemingly created to make the most of every view.

It is a surprisingly steep ascent to the Kleine Scheidegg. When you first look up at it from Grindelwald it is difficult to believe that there is a difference of more than a thousand metres of altitude, yet almost as soon as you leave Grund (in the bed of Grindelwald's valley) you will know that this is no gentle stroll. But look forward to the early part of the descent as far as Wengen, for that will be ample payment for the beads of sweat of the ascent.

At Alpiglen you're in the full aura of the Eiger, yet its north face is so close that you fail to gain a true perspective; every feature is distorted by foreshortening. However, once you reach Kleine Scheidegg this will be corrected, and from there you will also have a rewarding view of the Mönch and Jungfrau - two stunning mountains that threaten to push the Eiger into comparative obscurity as you descend towards Wengernalp.

Wengernalp will hold your attention and threaten to delay descent to

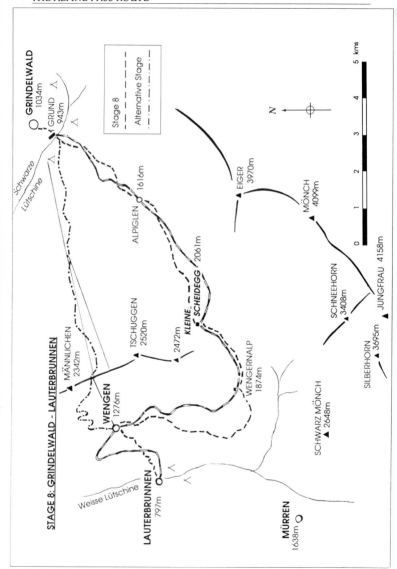

STAGE 8: GRINDELWALD – LAUTERBRUNNEN

Stage 8

Alternative Stage

N

0 1 2 3 4 5 kms

GRINDELWALD 1034m

GRUND 943m

Schwarze Lütschine

ALPIGLEN 1616m

EIGER 3970m

MÖNCH 4099m

SCHNEEHORN 3408m

JUNGFRAU 4158m

SILBERHORN 3695m

TSCHUGGEN 2520m

2472m

KLEINE SCHEIDEGG 2061m

WENGERNALP 1874m

SCHWARZ MÖNCH 2648m

MÄNNLICHEN 2342m

WENGEN 1276m

LAUTERBRUNNEN 797m

Weisse Lütschine

MÜRREN 1638m

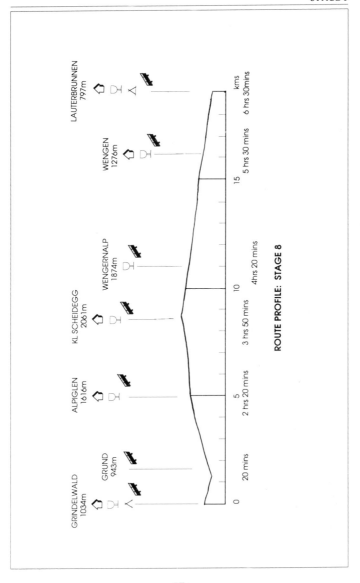

ROUTE PROFILE: STAGE 8

Lauterbrunnen. Not only are there superb views onto the Jungfrau, but also across the sudden depths of the Lauterbrunnen valley to the Gspaltenhorn and the mountains closing round above tomorrow's pass, the Sefinenfurke.

From Wengen itself a steep and twisting path takes you down into Lauterbrunnen - the valley of the waterfalls. By the time you reach it your knees will no doubt be aching, but there will be plenty to take your mind from any discomfort.

Note: A different crossing, which also leads from Grindelwald to Wengen and Lauterbrunnen, but via Männlichen, is described below as Alternative Stage 8.

※　　※　　※

From Grindelwald village station follow signs that direct you down to the station at Grund, where the train sets out for Kleine Scheidegg and the Jungfraujoch. By Grund station a signpost directs you onto a steep tarmac path (in fact a very narrow road) heading for Alpiglen and Kleine Scheidegg. It maintains its gradient nearly all the way to Alpiglen, but takes you past a number of lovely chalets and farms, through pastures and hay meadows, often parallel to the railway. When you pause for a breath you will see the Wetterhorn looking very impressive behind you, while the Eiger rises in grave solemnity over your left shoulder.

For the first hour you're on tarmac. Then through woods, past the station at **BRANDEGG** (1332m) and along a track to reach **ALPIGLEN** (1616m 2 hours 20 mins *accommodation, refreshments, railway*) where many north wall climbers have set out for the (1) Eiger. Seated at the hotel terrace there, a cool drink before you, is to be treated to a grandstand view overlooking the toy-like buildings of Grindelwald with the Wetterhorn towering over it from a pedestal of greenery.

The route continues, clearly marked and well-trodden, to take you beneath the Eiger's north face, the track less steep now, but with consistently fine views to enjoy as you wander up towards Kleine Scheidegg, whose large hotel buildings can soon be seen deceptively close. They will take you 1¹/₂ hours to reach from Alpiglen.

(2) **KLEINE SCHEIDEGG** (2061m 3 hours 50 mins *accommodation, refreshments, railway*) is invariably a-bustle with tourists having arrived there by train, either from Grindelwald or Wengen. It is here

*Kleine Scheidegg, a clutter of wires, hotels and station buildings
at the foot of the Eiger*

that the Jungfraujoch railway begins its journey, so it is an understandably busy place. There is generally someone here playing an alpenhorn to the bemusement and entertainment of visitors.

Cross the railway line to the left of the main station buildings and descend an easy track (signposted to Wengernalp and Wengen) at first right beside the railway with the Mönch and Jungfrau now dominating the scene. As far as Wengernalp station the track will no doubt be very busy. It also seems a little disappointing, especially with trains shuffling past, their overhead power lines detracting from the mountain ambience. But amends will soon be made.

Just short of the station at **WENGERNALP** (1874m 4 hours 20 mins *refreshments*) leave the main track and descend left on a narrow path over a steep and rough patch of pasture heading towards forest. Views from here are lovely. Continue with the path into the trees and come shortly to a track. This leads to an open alp with a truly spectacular panorama, not just of the shapely Jungfrau, but also of the Lauterbrunnen valley falling steeply below, the Breithorn at its head and the Gspaltenhorn opposite, forming a backing to Mürren.

We spread ourselves here to enjoy a late lunch, the sun warm on our faces, tent laid out to dry from last night's rain, bilberries fat and succulent on the low-growing shrubs that also had wild raspberries amongst them. It was peaceful there in the early afternoon, just a few dusty clouds hovering above the Silberhorn, and I recalled what Leslie Stephen had written in The Playground of Europe nearly a hundred years ago: "Surely the Wengern Alp must be precisely the loveliest place in this world." This was not quite the Wengernalp, but near enough to catch its echo. "It is delicious to lie upon the short crisp turf .... to watch a light summer mist driving by, and the great mountains look through its rents at intervals from an apparently impossible height above the clouds." That is precisely what we experienced, for there was no sense of urgency about the day. It was all downhill from here and I'd walked it often enough in the past to stroll down to Lauterbrunnen in the dark if need be. Then the peace was disturbed by a rumble and a roar, and pouring from the side of the Jungfrau was an avalanche. Long after its roar had cleared the air, powder snow continued to rain into a shallow gully. Barely had that ceased when another came, in a different place this time; then another and yet one more. Out of apparent stillness and calm there swept a

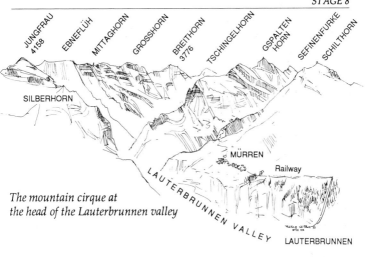

JUNGFRAU 4158 EBNEFLÜH MITTAGHORN GROSSHORN BREITHORN 3776 TSCHINGELHORN GSPALTEN HORN SEFINENFURKE SCHILTHORN

SILBERHORN

MÜRREN

Railway

*The mountain cirque at
the head of the Lauterbrunnen valley*

LAUTERBRUNNEN VALLEY

LAUTERBRUNNEN

white horror that, to us, at our safe distance, was but a source of entertainment. Easy to smile when you're not in its path, I thought.

The track leads on, winding easily round to the north now and gently making its descent to Wengen, first seen some way ahead and lying below on its green shelf nearly five hundred metres above the valley.

(3) **WENGEN** (1276m 5 hours 30 mins *accommodation, refreshments, shops, bank, PTT, railway*) is a popular resort with a justifiably famous panorama. The path down to Lauterbrunnen is signposted from the station. At first as a tarmac lane between trim-looking chalets, then a dirt path twisting interminably through trees with occasional views between them to the lovely Staubbach Falls cascading like a plume of smoke down the vertical walls that overshadow the village of **LAUTERBRUNNEN**.

(4) **LAUTERBRUNNEN** (797m 6 hours 30 mins) *Hotels, camping, restaurants, shops, banks, PTT, Postbus, railway (Kleine Scheidegg/Interlaken), funicular (Grütschalp/Mürren)*

Note: In view of the length of tomorrow's stage, and the fact that more than 1800 metres of height have to be gained to reach the

Sefinenfurke, it might be considered worthwhile continuing up to Mürren for the night - but only by funicular, or a combination of funicular (to Grütschalp) and footpath from there. (To walk all the way from Lauterbrunnen after having walked from Grindelwald is asking too much.) There is another reason why a night at or near Mürren might be worthwhile, and that is to catch the alpenglow setting the Jungfrau afire in the evening, and watching dawn rise over Eiger, Mönch and Jungfrau early next day. Note, though, that there are no campsites at Mürren, although there are two *matratzenlagers* offering modest accommodation half an hour above the village. See Stage 9 below for details.

Places Visited or Seen on the Way:

1. **THE EIGER:** This has passed into notoriety far beyond the limits of the mountaineering fraternity (for whom its horrors have faded somewhat) on account of the various tragedies that have been played out on its north face, mostly during the thirties. The mountain was first climbed (by its south-east flank) in 1858 by Charles Barrington with the guides Christian Almer and Peter Böhren; by the graceful knife-ridge of the Mittellegi in 1921 (by a Japanese, Yuko Maki and his guides), while the Nordwand was only won in 1938 by Harrer, Kasparek, Heckmair and Vörg. It has since been climbed in winter, solo, by siege tactics and in less than a day from the meadows at Alpiglen.

2. **KLEINE SCHEIDEGG:** Much-visited, much-publicised viewpoint which gazes onto Eiger, Mönch and Jungfrau, it is a major junction on the Wengen-Grindelwald-Jungfraujoch railway. As such it suffers from a rash of development not altogether in keeping with a high mountain environment. The first hotel was built here by Christian Seiler in 1834. (The Jungfraujoch railway was constructed between 1896-1912.)

3. **WENGEN:** Sitting on a comfortably wide terrace high above the Lauterbrunnen valley, Wengen is a popular and well-respected summer and winter resort with outstanding views over the classic U-shaped, glacier-carved valley, and to the Jungfrau, Mittaghorn,

Breithorn and Tschingelhorn at its head. On the wrong side of the valley to be useful as an overnight stop on the APR, its restaurants offer welcome refreshment.

4. **LAUTERBRUNNEN:** A straggling resort, situated in one of the narrowest stretches of the valley of the Weisse Lütschine, it takes its name from the many waterfalls that cascade down the almost vertical cliffs that line the valley. Its prettiest building is the church towards the southern end of the village. In the churchyard stands a bell that was brought over the glacier pass of Wetterlücke several centuries ago, in a mass migration from the Lötschental in canton Valais. There are two official campsites, both large and always extremely busy, but with first class facilities.

Monkshood

ALTERNATIVE STAGE 8:
GRINDELWALD - MÄNNLICHEN - WENGEN - LAUTERBRUNNEN

Distance:	16 kilometres
Time:	7 hours 40 mins
Start altitude:	1034m *High point:* Männlichen 2229m
Map:	L.S. 5004 Berner Oberland 1:50,000
Accommodation:	Männlichen (4 hours 20 mins) - Hotel
	Wengen (6 hours 20 mins) - Hotels
	Lauterbrunnen - Hotels, camping
Transport options:	Gondola lift (Grindelwald Grund - Männlichen)
	Cable-car (Männlichen - Wengen)
	Railway (Wengen - Lauterbrunnen)

This stage is a little longer than the main APR described above, and while Männlichen does not make such an obvious crossing as that of Kleine Scheidegg, this route has the advantage of taking you just far enough away from the Eiger to give a magnificent view of the mountain's great north face as you work your way up towards the Männlichen ridge.

This is not such a well-trodden route as that which leads over Kleine Scheidegg, and its only disadvantage is that there's mechanical uplift nearby. However, the sweeping pastures and glorious views more than compensate for this, and if you stray a little farther up the ridge to the easy summit of Männlichen, an even broader panorama is your reward, with the great trench of the Lauterbrunnen valley seen to dramatic effect.

The descent to Wengen is exceptionally steep at first, but is enlivened with the sight of parapente enthusiasts drifting colourfully overhead. (Männlichen is a popular launching site for these.) The Jungfrau appears larger than ever from the descent path, but it has to be said that the intimacy of Wengernalp is missing.

✳   ✳   ✳

From Grindelwald's main village railway station follow directions to Grund station in the valley below from where the Kleine Scheidegg/ Jungfraujoch railway sets out. Nearby a signpost gives directions to several places. Cross the river and follow a narrow tarmac road

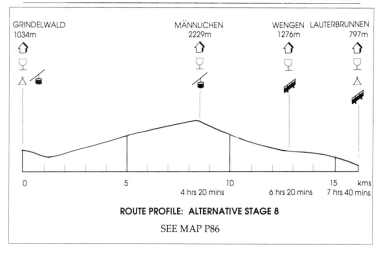

ROUTE PROFILE: ALTERNATIVE STAGE 8

SEE MAP P86

leading uphill among sloping pastures and neat chalets. The road leads to a footpath, rising steeply over more lush pastures. There will be a choice of paths, each one signposted and with times given to enable you to take that which suits.

As you continue uphill so views become more extensive. The Wetterhorn appears magnificent behind; the Eiger grows in stature and the Mönch and Jungfrau also show themselves in full snow-draped regalia.

A full description of the route would be superfluous; sufficient to say that you reach **HOLENSTEIN** (the middle station of the gondola lift) after about 2¹/₂ hours, **HINDER DER EGG** in 3 hours 10 minutes and the top station of the lift next to **MÄNNLICHEN HOTEL** (2229m *accommodation, refreshments*) about 4 hours 20 minutes after leaving Grindelwald.

Note: To walk up to the summit of (1) **MÄNNLICHEN** (2342m) will take about twenty minutes along a clear path.

A few metres north of the hotel, near the top station of the cable-car serving Wengen, the descent begins on an initially steep path which drops towards a number of avalanche fences. The path then cuts off north-westwards on a steady descent with the mountainside plunging steeply below. In places one gains a sense of exposure, but the path is in good condition and should be perfectly safe, although here and there it suddenly winds down in a series of tight zig-zags to test the knees. Views are consistently fine.

You lose sight of Wengen for a while as the way reaches woodland cover, but the route is always clear and obvious. Eventually it brings you out of the woods and along a track into (2) **WENGEN** (1276m 6 hours 40 mins *accommodation, refreshments, shops, banks, PTT, railway*).

Walk along the main street towards the railway station, and continue down a tarmac street (signposted to Lauterbrunnen) between chalets with fine views up to the Jungfrau hanging in the sky ahead. The street leads to a footpath which begins its steep zig-zag descent, heads into forest and eventually emerges on the edge of **LAUTERBRUNNEN**.

(3) **LAUTERBRUNNEN** (797m 7 hours 40 mins) *Hotels, camping, restaurants, shops, banks, PTT, Postbus, railway (Kleine Scheidegg/Interlaken), funicular (Grütschalp/Mürren).*

Note: Comments made at the end of Stage 8 (above) with regard to the possibility of continuing by funicular to Mürren in order to spend the night there to facilitate tomorrow's major crossing of the Sefinenfurke, are equally as valid here. Please refer to the note at the end of Stage 8.

❋ ❋ ❋

Places Visited on the Way:
1. **MANNLICHEN:** The culminating point on the ridge which separates the valleys of the Weisse Lütschine (Lauterbrunnen valley) and that of the Schwarze Lütschine (the valley of Grindelwald). This ridge folds gently towards Grindelwald, but falls steeply to Lauterbrunnen, relieved only by the broad shelf occupied by Wengen. The easy summit of Männlichen, at 2342 metres, gives a splendid panorama. North-westward lies Zweilütschinen at the confluence of the two valleys, with the Thunersee some distance beyond. To the east green pastures slide down to Grindelwald with the Wetterhorn rising magnificently and the savage blade of the Schreckhorn nearby. But it is to the south that one is tantalised by the Eiger, Mönch and

Blümlisalp, from the descent to Griesalp

Blümlisalp Glacier snout, below the Hohtürli (Stage 10)

Gsteig and Les Diablerets (Stage 14)

Jungfrau; the Mittaghorn and Grosshorn, elegant Breithorn and long spine of the Gspaltenhorn. A splendid panorama indeed.

2. **WENGEN:** See notes at the end of Stage 8 above.

3. **LAUTERBRUNNEN:** See notes at the end of Stage 8 above.

Field Gentian

STAGE 9:
LAUTERBRUNNEN - MÜRREN - SEFINENFURKE - GRIESALP

Distance:	21 kilometres
Time:	9 hours 15 mins
Start altitude:	797m *High point:* Sefinenfurke 2612m
Map:	L.S. 5004 Berner Oberland 1:50,000
Accommodation:	Mürren (2 hours 30 mins) - Hotels, matratzenlager
	Boggangen/Rotstock Hut (4 hours 40 mins) matratzenlager
	Obere Dürrenberg (7 hours 40 mins) - matratzenlager
	Griesalp - Hotel, matratzenlager
Transport option:	Funicular (Lauterbrunnen - Grütschalp - Mürren)

A hard day's walking, but a magnificent one. Sefinenfurke (also known as Sefinenfurgge) is all of 1800 metres above Lauterbrunnen; a fine pass, narrow, rocky and remote. To reach it entails a long approach over a series of undulating grasslands and along the edge of the steeply sloping, but minor peak of Brünli. But first you must climb out of Lauterbrunnen's deep cleft, and this makes for a demanding start to the day. If you are travelling light then the route is acceptable in its entirety. If, however, you are heavily laden, it may be as well to consider the alternatives available.

The funicular from Lauterbrunnen to Mürren would save some 2¹/₂hours of severe uphill effort, and thereby make the remainder of the walk a little less demanding. For those unhappy with the thought of this amount of mechanical aid, a compromise might be to take the funicular up the steepest part of the climb, that is, as far as Grütschalp, and walk from there. (Mürren is reached in 1 hour 10 minutes from Grütschalp, thus saving almost 1 ¹/₂hours on the day's overall time.) Having personally walked the complete route and on a separate occasion taken the funicular to Grütschalp and walked from there, I would favour the latter option.

From the pass the descent to Griesalp is severe. It is extremely steep in places - in fact there are 1200 metres of height to lose in about 5¹/₂ kilometres - but the path is always clear and easily found. Griesalp itself is a small hamlet almost entirely given over to accommodation for walkers and climbers. *There is no campsite.*

On this stage of the walk there are many wonderful views to enjoy. At first they are dominated by the peaks at the head of Lauterbrunnen's valley. Then it is the Gspaltenhorn that holds your attention before you head into a rough region of pasture, cupped by lesser mountain heights and with the Schilthorn above to the right. The Sefinenfurke's best views are back the way you have come, with the Eiger and Mönch seen side-on, but as you descend towards Griesalp, so the huge mass of the Blümlisalp shows itself in full majesty. A demanding day's walk, but a scenic one. It'll be a day to remember.

* * *

Main APR: (Lauterbrunnen-Mürren)
The path to Mürren begins near a bakery in Lauterbrunnen's street a short distance up-valley from the railway station and is, of course, well signposted. It climbs very steeply, mostly in forest, then swings left and eases a little to make a steadily rising traverse of the hillside.

The Jungfrau, seen from the path to Mürren

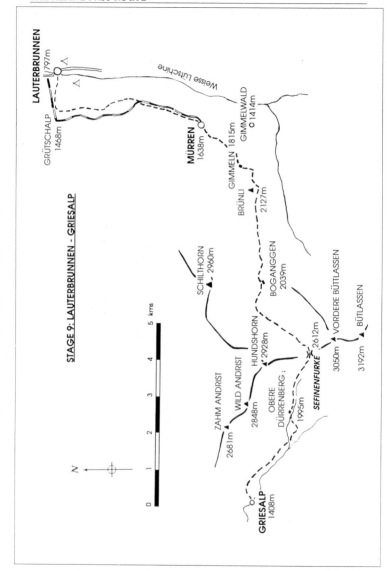

STAGE 9: LAUTERBRUNNEN - GRIESALP

LAUTERBRUNNEN
797m

GRÜTSCHALP
1468m

Weisse Lütschine

MÜRREN
1638m

GIMMELN 1815m

GIMMELWALD 1414m

BRÜNLI
2127m

BOGANGGEN
2039m

SCHILTHORN
2960m

HUNDSHORN
2928m

VORDERE BÜTLASSEN
3050m

ZAHM ANDRIST
2681m

WILD ANDRIST
2848m

OBERE
DÜRRENBERG
1995m

SEFINENFURKE
2612m

BÜTLASSEN
3192m

N

GRIESALP
1408m

0 1 2 3 4 5 kms

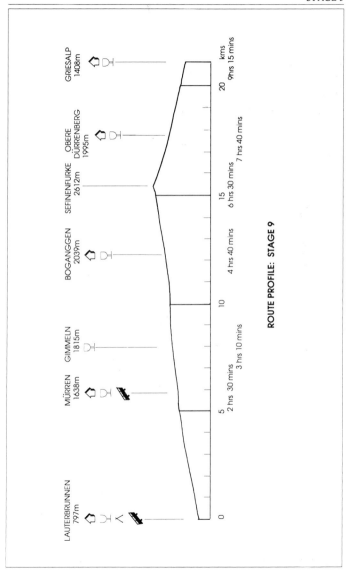

ROUTE PROFILE: STAGE 9

Whenever there are path junctions a signpost will be found to direct you along the correct trail. After nearly two hours the path brings you out of the forest and onto the level of the railway line, which you then follow all the way to (1) **MÜRREN** (1638m 2 hours 30 mins *accommodation, refreshments, shops, bank, PTT*).

Alternative Route: (Lauterbrunnen-Grütschalp-Mürren)
Take the Lauterbrunnen/Mürren funicular as far as Grütschalp (at the top of the steep incline above the valley). On leaving Grütschalp station cross the railway track and follow a clear path heading to the left, signposted to Mürren. When the path forks soon after, continue ahead along the lower trail. No further description is necessary since the way is obvious and adequately signposted. Sufficient to say that it becomes scenically delightful - especially with views to the Jungfrau where you can see the whole spectacular height and depth of the mountain, from summit to valley floor all 3200 metres of it; one of the biggest mountain precipices in Europe. At **WINTEREGG** (1578m) refreshments are available at a restaurant beside the railway.

Note: If you have journeyed to Mürren intending to spend the night here prior to crossing the Sefinenfurke, it should be borne in mind that this resort's hotels tend towards the expensive. Alternatives to consider are the Youth Hostel in nearby Gimmelwald, or two *matratzenlagers* 30 minutes above Mürren. If you choose one of the latter follow the Alternative Route via Suppenalp outlined below.

Alternative Route: (Mürren-Suppenalp-Boganggen)
From the railway station on the outskirts of Mürren take the upper, right-hand road leading into the village and walk along the continuing street until you come to the Schilthorn cable-car station. Just above this you will find a footpath climbing steeply on the left-hand side of a stream (direction Suppenalp). It maintains its steep climb above the village, alongside pastures and through patches of woodland, to arrive in 30 minutes at **SUPPENALP** (1852m *Berghaus/ matratzenlager, restaurant*). *(The other matratzenlager, Pension Sonnenberg, will be found by taking the footpath beyond Suppenalp, then bear right towards Almendhübel.)*

From Suppenalp, where there are outstanding views across the

Half an hour above Mürren Berghaus Suppenalp
offers matratzenlager accommodation

valley to the Jungfrau - especially fine on a summer's evening when the snows catch the last glow of sunset, and to watch daybreak over the Mönchjoch - bear left on the path signposted to Schiltalp. The path rises across a vegetated hillside, passes beneath the Schilthorn cableway and rounds a bluff to be greeted by the wonderful sight of the Gspaltenhorn in the south sending out its monstrous ridge, suitably glazed with ice, on the far side of the Sefinental.

A high pastureland then leads to **SCHILTALP** (1951m 30 mins from Suppenalp), a small hamlet of cheesemakers' huts where there is a junction of tracks. Continue straight ahead for Boganggen (in 1 hour 20 mins) and Sefinenfurke (in 3 hours 20 mins).

A few metres beyond Schiltalp a narrow path breaks away from the track and goes half-left ahead, contours round the hillside and after about 10 minutes reaches another junction of paths by a stream flowing through the Schiltal. (High above can be seen the (2) Schilthorn.) Cross the stream and climb steeply on a path among lush, dank vegetation, emerging at the top of a narrow green ridge with more fine views all around.

Continue on the far side by descending in a steady traverse to reach a broad pastureland with a Bergweg signpost directing to Oberlager, Boganggen, Sefinenfurke and Griesalp (reached in 4 hours 30 mins). You have now rejoined the main trail of the Alpine Pass Route. Follow this path round the hillside heading west for a further 25 minutes to reach **BOGANGGEN/ROTSTOCK HUT** (2039m *accommodation, refreshments*).

Main APR: (Mürren-Gimmeln-Boganggen)
From Mürren railway station take the lower of two roads ahead and walk along the village street, passing hotels, shops and private houses all enjoying the same magnificent views. At the southern end of the village wander uphill along a tarmac path between meadows and follow signs for Schonegg and Gimmeln. Not only is the Breithorn looking superb at the head of the valley from here, but the Gspaltenhorn is particularly impressive.

Beyond the farm buildings of **GIMMELN** (1815m 3 hours 10 mins) cross the Schiltbach and pass beside a small restaurant, heading south. The path brings you to a spur of mountain (the minor peak of **BRÜNLI** [2127m]) and then veers right to climb the spur itself. This is a steep, but short climb that soon eases to pass along the left-hand side of the peak.

When I first came along here it was with a group on a bright summer's day, and we decided to rest for a few minutes to enjoy the sunshine, the glorious views, the stillness and the overpowering sense of peace. There was just the lightest of breezes and practically nothing stirred. Only out of far distance was there to be heard the merest hint of a waterfall pouring down an unseen wall. No-one spoke and each was left to his own thoughts. But suddenly the peace was broken by a loud yodel - and it came from directly above. We looked up, startled, to find a gaily-coloured parachute drifting gently overhead! The man dangling from it had obviously come from the Schilthorn where parapente enthusiasts amuse themselves by leaping off the mountain and sailing the breezes down to the Lauterbrunnen valley. Surely, I pondered, this must be the ultimate laxative.

*Gspaltenhorn, a superb mountain, seen from the meadows
outside Mürren*

The path now contours across a large area of pasture, grazed in summer by cattle, and leads directly to a farm building next to the Rotstock Hut which belongs to the Stechelberg Ski Club. This is shown on the map as **BOGANGGEN** (2039m 4 hours 40 mins, *accommodation, refreshments*).

Ahead lies a large bowl of rough pastureland pocked with boulders, on the far western side of which the final ascent to the pass begins. The way leads through a contorted landscape with the Sefinenfurke seen above on an interesting rocky ridge. Heading up towards it seems to be a long, slow process. The last part of the climb involves ascending a steep zig-zag path on a slope of gritty black scree, broken here and there by rocks. But the pass itself is rewarding. **SEFINENFURKE** (2612m 6 hours 30 mins) is a narrow, craggy pass slung between the Hundshorn to the north and Büttlassen to the south. (This latter peak is connected to the Gspaltenhorn by a short ridge.) Views back to the Eiger and Mönch are particularly fine, while

Descent from the Sefinenfurke

the glacier-hung massif of the Blümlisalp rises a comparatively short distance away in the south-west.

Immediately below the pass on the western side the initial slope is safeguarded by a fixed rope hand rail. The path is somewhat tortuous in its twisting on more gritty scree, but it soon cuts across towards the right where the descent is a little easier. Below the screes you come to grassy hillocks and a small stream breaking through a gully to your left. The path follows the stream down, and a little over an hour from the pass you come to **OBERE DÜRRENBERG** (1995m 7 hours 40 mins *accommodation, refreshments*), a small farm building squatting on the right bank of the stream. Just below this cross to the left bank where the path winds down a steep hillside of grass with fine views up to the Blümlisalp which looks imposing, large and powerful in the south. Also seen across the valley of the Gamchi are the farm buildings of Untere and Oberi Bund, appearing small and remote on a high ledge of hillside. These will be visited on the next stage of the walk on the way to Hohtürli.

Eventually the path brings you to a small farm, **BURGLI** (1620m), at a junction of valleys. Bear right here across a stream, and follow the farm road which then leads down towards Griesalp.

Note: If you have started the day's walk from Mürren, it is possible that you will have the time and inclination to shorten tomorrow's crossing by avoiding the descent into Griesalp and going up to Oberi Bund where *matratzenlager* accommodation is to be had. If so, follow Alternative Route directions below.

Alternative Route: (Burgli-Oberi Bund [Bundalp])
Walk down the farm road a short distance, keeping alert for a footpath signposted to Griesalp that breaks away on the left-hand side of the road and heads towards forest. Soon another path leads off from this, also to the left (signposted Hohtürli and Blümlisalphütte). It crosses an open grassland, goes over a footbridge and begins to climb steeply up a hillside again and into woods. The path retains its steep gradient for a while among the trees and then emerges onto another farm road, this one having come from Griesalp. Nearby is the alp of **UNTERE BUND** (1698m). Where the road bends to the right the continuing path cuts straight ahead up the hillside towards a hinted shelf of pasture, and takes you directly to **OBERI BUND** (1840m 1 hour 10 mins from Burgli; *accommodation, refreshments*). Next to it is another Berghaus owned by the Swiss Alpine Club with more accommodation.

Main APR: (Burgli-Griesalp)
Remain on the farm road all the way from Burgli. It soon leads through very pleasant country, green and lush and pastoral, passes through the pretty hamlet of **STEINENBERG** (1463m 9 hours), continues ahead with the Kiental seen cutting a long swathe through the mountains to the north-west, then swings left to descend into **GRIESALP**.

(3) **GRIESALP** (1408m 9 hours 15 mins) *Hotel, matratzenlager, shop, Postbus (Griesalp-Kiental)*

Places Visited or Seen on the Way:

1. **MÜRREN:** A much-favoured resort enjoying some of the loveliest views of any village in the Alps, it is the highest permanently inhabited village in the Bernese Oberland. In common with Wengen across the valley, Mürren is spared the motor car and there are no roads to it, most visitors approaching by funicular to Grütschalp and train from there. The village was first recorded in the thirteenth century as *Mons Mürren*. In the first half of the 19th century it was visited by several notable Englishmen, including John Addington Symonds and Lord Tennyson, but it was Arnold Lunn who accelerated its all-year round popularity when he invented the modern slalom here in 1922. Two years later he founded the Kandahar Ski Club at the Palace Hotel. A memorial stone dedicated to Lunn stands in a small garden by the railway station.

Memorial to
Sir Arnold Lunn
at Mürren

2. **THE SCHILTHORN:** This easy peak (2960m) has long made a popular ascent on account of its accessibility and the extent of its summit panorama. There is now a cable-car to the top where a revolving restaurant has just been enlarged to accommodate the vast number of visitors who daily throng there. (This featured in the James Bond film, *On Her Majesty's Secret Service*, in which the mountain was renamed Piz Gloria.) In 1865, Alice Arbuthnot was struck by lightning near the little Grausee tarn (between the Schilthorn and Birg) whilst on her honeymoon. A monument recalls the incident. The first 'Inferno' ski race from the summit to Lauterbrunnen took place in 1928.

3. **GRIESALP:** A tiny hamlet ranged around a square at the end of a narrow toll road that rises through the gentle valley of Kiental. Specially-built small Postbuses serve it from Kiental village. Griesalp makes a fine base for a walking, climbing or ski-mountaineering holiday.

GRIESALP - HÖHTURLI - KANDERSTEG

Distance:	15 kilometres
Time:	7 hours 30 mins
Start altitude:	1408m *High point:* Hohtürli 2778m
Map:	L.S. 5004 Berner Oberland 1:50,000
Accommodation:	Oberi Bund (1 hour 15 mins) - Matratzenlager
	Blümlisalphütte (4 hours 30 mins) - SAC hut
	Oeschinensee (6 hours 30 mins) - Hotels,
	gasthof/matratzenlager
	Kandersteg - Hotels, gasthof, camping
Transport option:	Chair-lift (Oeschinensee - Kandersteg)

*Hohtürli is the highest point on the Alpine Pass Route, and its crossing one
of the most demanding. However, that being said, it is one to look forward
to and to enjoy - not only in retrospect, but during the event. The route is a
varied one. It begins with a woodland walk. Then comes an easy farm road
winding among pastures to lull you into a false sense of complacency.
Suddenly the upward climb begins with a vengeance; up a steep spur of scree
to a minor ridge. Beyond that comes a gentle traverse before the path rears
again in a series of zig-zags beside a slightly overhanging rock wall. The pass
is reached with a welcome surprise, and the Blümlisalphütte stands just far
enough above it to entice with its promise of refreshments.*

*Hohtürli gives a grandstand view of some wild high mountain scenery. As
wild as anything yet seen since leaving Sargans. To one side the glaciers of
the Blümlisalp massif hang suspended from their individual crests, while far
away Kandersteg's valley is but a shadow to lure you down. The descent is
first on scree, then along an ancient moraine running beside the snouts of
glaciers and into a grassy basin. It is with some degree of pleasure that you
then find yourself peering into the great fjord-like shaft that holds the
Oeschinensee, while the path takes you down towards it to a romantically
situated alp, before veering off to find a belvedere of a trail running round
the face of a mountain high above the lake's northern shore. Finally the
descent into Kandersteg is by way of an extremely steep but narrow tarmac
road. Down among waterfalls, shrubs and trees. Down to a little resort that
straggles along the valley.*

The Hohtürli path above Oberi Bund

* * *

To the side of Berghaus Griesalp a signpost marks the start of the route to Hohtürli and sends you up into forest shade. Path leads to track and onto a farm road winding steadily up along the edge of the woods and through pastures with the high peaks frowning overhead. At **UNTER BUND** (1698m) leave the road and head steeply up a grassy path towards a shelf of pasture hinted above. You come back onto the road again and soon afterwards reach **OBERI BUND** (1840m 1 hour 15 mins *accommodation, refreshments*).

Continue along the road for a few hundred metres more as it winds into an upper region of rucked pasture. A signpost here intimates the way forward. A path heads up and across these pastures and onto a steep slope of moraine deposits, partially grassed over. The path fights a way up a spur of black grit, and as you work ever higher so the slope seems to grow even more severe - but you have the bonus of gaining valuable height with practically every step. There are a few zig-zags, but weather erosion forestalls any long-term pathway, and you can see great runnels and gullies washed out by spring thaw and heavy rain.

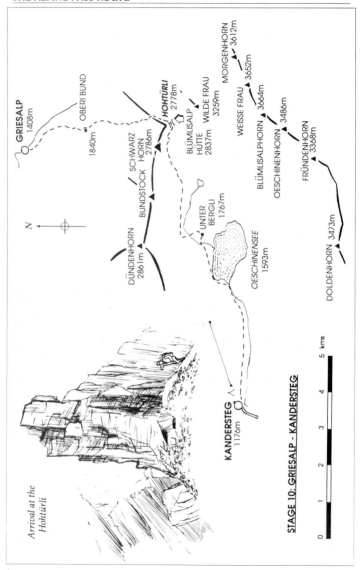

GRIESALP 1408m

OBERI BUND

1840m

SCHWARZ HORN 2786m

HOHTÜRLI 2778m

BLÜMLISALP HÜTTE 2837m

WILDE FRAU 3259m

MORGENHORN 3612m

WEISSE FRAU 3652m

BLÜMLISALPHORN 3664m

OESCHINENHORN 3486m

FRÜNDENHORN 3368m

DOLDENHORN 3473m

BUNDSTOCK

DÜNDENHORN 2861m

UNTER BERGLI 1767m

OESCHINENSEE 1593m

N

KANDERSTEG 1176m

Arrival at the Hohtürli

STAGE 10: GRIESALP - KANDERSTEG

0   1   2   3   4   5 kms

112

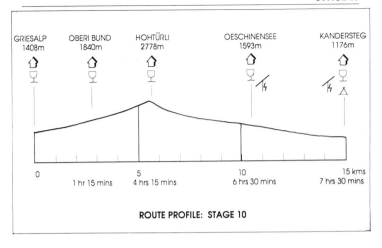

ROUTE PROFILE: STAGE 10

Although lightly laden the first time I came this way I found the path extremely unpleasant and tiring, and for days leading up to the second crossing a year later (this time with a much more substantial rucksack on my back) I privately dreaded this section. However, it was not half as bad as I'd remembered and I actually found it rather enjoyable despite the clouds draped in white wreaths below and the heavy sky above. There were others coming down too, including a pair of priests looking most uncomfortable in their long black cassocks and dog collars, who told us they'd spent the night in the Blümlisalphütte and were then on their way to Mürren by way of the Sefinenfurke - reversing our route. I was reminded then of tales from the days of Alpine pioneering when some of the earliest high mountain journeys were actually carried out by clerics on their way to conduct services in some far outpost of Christianity. It was as though for a moment we too had stepped back a hundred years and more, for there was little outwardly of these two priests to suggest the twentieth century.

Eventually the black moraine slope ends on a grey rock ridge, and paint marks lead you on a steady rising traverse of it before tucking against its left-hand side where the path eases above long slips of snow. Hohtürli is now directly above, but unseen as yet. The path continues on and begins to climb by a series of rocky shelves, then steep zig-zags aided by chains and lengths of fixed cable. At last you catch sight of the Blümlisalphütte above you on the skyline with a sense of relief at prospects of soon rising onto the pass.

HÖHTURLI (2778m 4 hours 15 mins) lies a little below the **BLÜMLISALPHUTTE** (2837m *accommodation, refreshments*) and it is worth wandering up the last few metres to it for a bowl of hot soup or a drink. This hut was substantially refurbished in 1988/89 and is now superbly equipped. Views from it are extraordinarily fine, with the glaciers of the (1) Blümlisalp (Morgenhorn and Weisse Frau) draped close by. Long views are also given out to the west where a complex of ridges confuse tomorrow's route.

The way down to Kandersteg is on a clearly marked path, initially on well-graded zig-zags over long broad slopes of scree, then on a balcony looking across to the left where glacial tongues hang obscenely above cold-looking depths. Then comes a moraine wall with the path balanced along its crest, and eventually veering to the right into a rough bowl of pasture dotted with boulders and with a stream winding through. Several huts are sunken into this undulating ground, almost overshadowed by the huge boulders. This is **OBER BERGLI** (1973m 5 hours 45 mins).

A few moments later you gaze steeply down into the fjord-like basin of the (2) Oeschinensee, and the path takes you to it by way of a well-made stairway of a path. At the foot of this descent you come to the alp of **UNTER BERGLI** (1767m) where you bear right, cross a stream by way of a footbridge, and follow the continuing path that leads along the right-hand side of the lake, but some way above it.

It was the end of summer and all the cattle and goats were being driven from the alps where they'd been grazing since June, down to the lowlands. The lead cows had their heads adorned with flowers and wreaths and with tiny trees fixed to their horns. They led the procession with a strange kind of bovine dignity, while one or two of the goats played truant and tried to escape by climbing above the path. A well-aimed stone from one of the herders marked the error of their ways and they returned to their rightful place towards the back of the line. We strolled behind them, unable to overtake, walking on a moist brown carpet all the way to the lake's end.

*On the long descent from Hohtürli the APR skirts Oeschinensee,
one of the best-loved lakes in the Bernese Oberland*

Towards the western end of the lake the path slopes down and takes you among trees, then round to a collection of buildings above the **OESCHINENSEE** (1593m 6 hours 30 mins; *accommodation, refreshments*) where a narrow road will be found which leads to Kandersteg. It's a steep road in places, used only by service vehicles for the hotels at the lake, and is invariably busy with holiday-makers wandering back to Kandersteg. On the way down there are several waterfalls seen off to the left spraying into the valley. After about an hour's walking from the lake you arrive in **KANDERSTEG**.

(3) **KANDERSTEG** (1176m 7 hours 30 mins) *Hotels, gasthofs, camping, shops, banks, PTT, Postbus, railway (Kandersteg - Spiez/Thun/ Goppenstein)*

✻ ✻ ✻

Places Visited or Seen on the Way:
1. **BLÜMLISALP:** A fine, bold and snowy mountain massif, it dominates the whole walk from Griesalp to Kandersteg. It has a number of summits, all with hanging glaciers on their northern flanks and short, but steep walls dropping to the icefield of the Kanderfirn to the south. Highest summit of the massif is the Blümlis-alphorn (3664m), first climbed by Leslie Stephen, with R Liveing and J K Stone and their guides in August 1860. Next is the Weisse Frau (3652m), then the Morgenhorn (3612m) directly above the Blümlisalp hut.

2. **OESCHINENSEE:** This is one of the most notable mountain lakes in Switzerland; a beautiful oval sheet of water cupped in a great scoop of mountains. The peaks of the Blümlisalp and Fründenhorn rise abruptly from its shoreline, while the western end is marked by a patch of forest and high pastures. There are two hotels and a berghaus nearby, offering plenty of accommodation, including *matratzenlager*.

3. **KANDERSTEG:** Noted as a mountaineering centre for a hundred years and more, this medium-sized resort is also ideally situated as a base for a walking holiday. There is much fine scenery on all sides, some delightful accessible valleys, high passes to cross (glaciated and otherwise) and a number of mountain huts placed within a few hours' walk of the town centre. The railway is very busy here for it is

on a major international line using the Lötschberg Tunnel (nearly 15 kilometres long) on its traverse of the Alps. There are a number of useful shops (groceries, photographic, bookshops etc.) including a hardware store which stocks paraffin, meths etc. for use with certain types of camping stove. There is a major International Scout Camp in Kandersteg, and one public campsite situated on the eastern edge of town, at the foot of the Oeschinensee chair-lift.

STAGE 11:
KANDERSTEG - BUNDERCHRINDE - ADELBODEN

Distance:	16 kilometres
Time:	6 hours 45 mins
Start altitude:	1176m *High point:* Bunderchrinde 2385m
Map:	L.S. 5009 Gstaad-Adelboden 1:50,000
Accommodation:	Bonderalp (5 hours) - matratzenlager
	Adelboden - Hotels, gasthof, camping
Transport option:	Cable-car (Kandersteg - Allmenalp)

Bunderchrinde is a classic pass, a mere nick in the high wall of mountains running round from the Gross Lohner to the Allmegrat. Views on the way to it include, spectacularly, the Gasterntal cutting into the mountains to the east, while from the pass itself the western outlook is equally grand.

The ascent route makes its way in steps. First there is an easy valley walk, then a steep woodland climb to gain access to the Usser Ueschene valley where you can enjoy another gentle stroll before rising steeply again, this time to overcome a long line of slabs and cliffs. Once above these you traverse a wild and lonely shelf of hillside and then tackle the final scree slope that takes you to the Bunderchrinde. The downward path similarly drops in steps and takes almost as long to complete as does the upward section of the walk.

This is the last of the major passes that will need to be crossed on the APR, although there are other days that will be as demanding as this. It takes you away from the big Oberland peaks towards a more tolerant landscape, where the mountains smile benevolently and pastures are lush and flower-decked in early summer.

✳   ✳   ✳

The route begins near Kandersteg railway station where a signpost directs you left along a tarmac footpath following the railway line. The path soon veers right under a bridge, crosses the River Kander and continues ahead now along a narrow road towards the landing site of Kandersteg's paragliding school. Here you have a choice of routes; one which is the main APR, the other which gives the opportunity to gain more than 500 metres of height by mechanical

118

means, followed by a scenic belvedere path.

Alternative Route (via cable-car to Allmenalp):
The narrow road swings right and comes to a halt by the Kandersteg - Allmenalp cable-car station. Take the cableway to Allmenalp, walk a short distance above the upper station and then at a signpost bear left on a footpath leading to an alpine chalet where cheese is made on the premises. (*Refreshments available.*) The path continues in a rough southerly direction, climbs briefly then becomes a broad track contouring round the mountainside, with magnificent views to the Blümlisalp off to the left, and to the Balmhorn and Altels directly ahead. It's an easy track, gentle on the legs, and after passing the few alp buildings of **RYHARD** you soon come to the entrance of the lovely Ueschinen valley. Remain with the track heading into the valley until you come to a junction at **AEUSSER UESCHINEN** (1595m) where you rejoin the main route and walk up-valley.

Main APR:
At the paragliding landing site a footpath goes ahead from the road, leading you up-valley alongside the river, and brings you to the International Scout Camp building - **PFADFINDER ZENTRUM** (1185m 30 mins). Just beyond the buildings a footpath breaks away to the right (signposted to Bunderchrinde and Adelboden), and crosses two or three open meadows.

On coming to another signpost midway across one of these meadows where the footpath forks, take the right branch which will take you into woods. The ascent begins with the path climbing steeply through the woods. Across a road continue ahead through more woodland and come onto the road again. Follow the road for a short distance (it winds in long loops up the hillside to enter the Usser Ueschine valley), then take the waymarked short-cut heading alongside the Alpbach stream - but keep alert for a fork in the path where you must cut away to the right and climb up to the road once more. A few metres beyond this you enter the Usser Ueschine valley.

Continue along the road into this shallow pastoral valley, until you come to **AEUSSER UESCHINEN** (1595m 1 hour 45 mins) - a small cluster of farm buildings where the road forks. Head to the left,

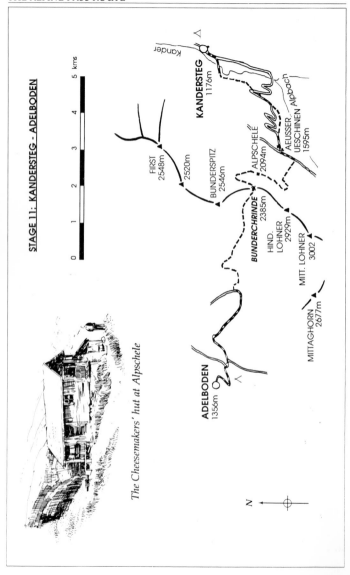

STAGE 11: KANDERSTEG - ADELBODEN

Kander

KANDERSTEG
1176m

AEUSSER
UESCHINEN Alpbach
1595m

ALPSCHELE
2094m

FIRST
2548m

BUNDERSPITZ
2546m

BUNDERCHRINDE
2385m

HIND.
LOHNER
2929m

MITT. LOHNER
3002

MITTAGHORN
2677m

ADELBODEN
1356m

N

0   1   2   3   4   5 kms

The Cheesemakers' hut at Alpschele

120

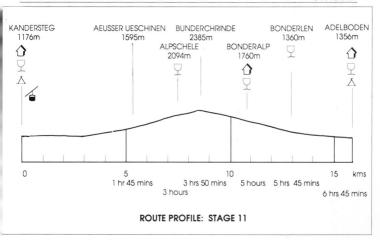

ROUTE PROFILE: STAGE 11

aiming deeper into the valley, but after about 400 metres leave the valley road and take the footpath seen to the right heading up a stony hillside towards a fine band of grey cliffs. The path gains height with economy, swings left and then climbs beside a stream, seeking a fault line up the cliffs. Then across the stream, zig-zagging steeply again before heading to the right over boulder slopes. (Good views off to the right into the (1) Gasterntal.)

Eventually you come to three rough huts, **ALPSCHELE** (2094m 3 hours, *refreshments*) where you gain the first view of Bunderchrinde above.

Treading knee-high clouds and cold rain two of us arrived here one day and were invited inside to dry off. We were given tall glasses of milky coffee by the cheesemakers living here for the summer and so, remembering them with affection, the following year when I returned I remained hopeful of a similar welcome. But this time summer was virtually over and the cheesemakers had gone down to the valley. My heart fell. In their place were two chamois hunters who sympathised with us (it was a cold, blustery day), and who were every bit as hospitable as their predecessors. For they presented us with bowls of what they called Jäger Kaffee (Hunters' Coffee - milk coffee laced with apfelschnapps) to warm us up. It was most effective, and when we set off again along the path there was a healthy glow colouring our cheeks.

From Alpschele the path continues over grass slopes with a green saddle seen ahead, then winds back to the left and comes to a signpost on the edge of a broad slope of scree. The path rises at a comforting angle across the scree, and brings you directly to the pass of **BUNDERCHRINDE** (2385m 3 hours 50 mins).

It is a splendid narrow gash of a pass between brash walls of rock. Savour it. Two paths lead from it. The Adelboden route drops steeply, while a second route heads off to the right (north) to Bunderspitz (in 40 minutes) for a circular walk which continues down to Allmenalp and back to Kandersteg again. Far below you can see Adelboden.

The descent is made by a series of long zig-zags down more screes towards a grassy bluff at the foot of a stone-scooped corrie. A small cattle byre is found here. The path descends to the left of this and soon divides. (Both routes lead to Adelboden.) Take the right-hand option. It leads over a rough pastureland to a farm, then down below it to a farm road where you turn right. You will shortly reach another building, **BONDERALP** (1760m 5 hours *matratzenlager, refreshments*) where there are more route decisions to be made.

Either continue along the road, which will twist down to Adelboden in 1 hour 40 minutes; or take the footpath from Bonderalp which cuts away to the left and also takes 1 hour 40 minutes to reach Adelboden. Since the road route needs no description, the way by footpath is outlined below.

The path cuts back to the left and swings its way across meadows towards yet another farmhouse, then enters forest. Waymarks lead in and out of the trees, cutting across the road here and there and finally coming onto the road through the valley of the Bunderle Bach (refreshments available at one or two trim restaurants). Without any difficulties you should arrive on the edge of Adelboden near a timber yard. On reaching another road bear right towards a garage, then left at the junction to walk uphill into **ADELBODEN**, passing within a few metres of a campsite on your left.

(2) **ADELBODEN** (1356m 6 hours 45 mins) *Hotels, gasthof, camping, shops, banks, PTT, bus (Adelboden - Frutigen)*

Places Visited or Seen on the Way:

1. **GASTERNTAL:** Branching off to the east at the head of the Kandertal the Gasterntal is a glorious, steep-walled valley sliced by meandering streams born among either the Kanderfirn glacier, or by the numerous waterfalls that streak the great rock faces. There are no villages in the valley, just a couple of hotels and a handful of farm buildings, but it is an enchanting place well worth a visit given sufficient days to spare.

2. **ADELBODEN:** A summer and winter resort perched on a high terrace with a splendid view of the snowy Wildstrubel to the south. Adelboden is situated at the junction of several tributary valleys, the best of which is that of the Engstligenalp whose fine waterfall can be seen from the village. As a resort it tends to be a little more expensive than some, but there are plenty of shops for restocking supplies.

   Note: If you are camping it will not be necessary to go all the way up into the village, as tomorrow's route begins midway between the campsite (note above) and Adelboden proper. There is a foodstore near to the campsite if required.

The Bunderchrinde from Adelboden

ADELBODEN - HAHNENMOOS - LENK

Distance:	14 kilometres
Time:	4 hours 30 mins
Start altitude:	1356m *High point:* Hahnenmoos 1956m
Map:	L.S. 5009 Gstaad-Adelboden 1:50,000
Accommodation:	Gilbach (40 mins) - Gasthof, matratzenlager
	Hahnenmoos (2 hours 45 mins) - Hotel, matratzenlager
	Büelberg (3 hours 25 mins) - Gasthof
	Lenk - Hotels, gasthof, camping
	(at Oberried, 4 kms to the south)
Transport options:	Bus (Adelboden-Geilsbuel)
	Gondola lift (Geilsbuel-Hahnemoos)
	Bus (Büelberg-Lenk)

This is one of the easiest and least demanding of all APR stages which will allow the opportunity to wander unfussed through the gentle valley of the Geilsbach, and over the Hahnemoos Pass, without any undue exertion. Much of it is along narrow surfaced roads; the uphill stretch from Geilsbuel to the pass being accompanied by brightly-coloured gondolas swinging overhead.

An alternative route to Lenk, which maintains the spirit of the long walk, crosses the neighbouring Pommernpass and descends by way of the Simmen Falls. It is a little more strenuous than the main route. (See Alternative Route 12 for details.)

✳   ✳   ✳

If you have stayed overnight in Adelboden proper, as opposed to camping on the approach to it, walk through the town heading south-west along the main street, soon leaving shops and hotels behind. When the road forks, continue ahead along the left branch. This soon crosses the river and twists into the Geilsbach valley bringing you to a number of scattered buildings at **GILBACH** (1431m 40 mins; *accommodation, refreshments*) where you enjoy some pleasant pastoral views.

If, however, you have spent the night at the campsite on the outskirts of Adelboden, it is not necessary to walk up into the town. Instead, wander a short distance uphill alongside the main road to the first hairpin bend. Leave the road here and continue straight ahead to pass alongside a soft drinks factory (*Mineralquelle*) where a signpost indicates the start of the route to Hahnenmoos. Follow the tarmac path/narrow road which soon breaks away to the left to cross the Allebach. The way divides. Continue to follow the river and you will soon curve left to enter the Geilsbach valley and join the main route.

Keep along the road as it heads deeper into the valley. It is rather more enjoyable than you might anticipate, for the valley is green and welcoming and the mountains ahead wear a benevolent smile. There are no gaunt faces to glower under a grey sky, nor scree slopes to tackle on a tight zig-zag path. You can swing along without a regular consultation with the map and make good time - if that is your wish. If not, then this is a valley to stroll through at a leisurely pace.

When the road forks about 1.5 kilometres south of Gilbach, take the right-hand road, and 500 metres later where it makes a sharp hairpin bend, leave the road and follow a footpath ahead through woods. It leads directly to **GEILSBUEL** (1720m 2 hours; *refreshments, gondola lift*) with the saddle of Hahnenmoos above. Continue up to the pass using short-cuts where possible, but the road where not. It will demand no more than about 45 minutes.

HAHNENMOOS (1956m 2 hours 45 mins; *accommodation, refreshments*) is a very busy place. On a fine day it can be as crowded as Grosse Scheidegg or the Klausenpass, on account of its accessibility, but the views are lovely and they include the wall of mountains to the east where yesterday's pass is hidden.

Alternative Route: (Hahnenmoos-Lenk)
The advantage of this alternative is that you have a more interesting descent to Lenk with a visit to the fine Simmenfälle (waterfalls). The disadvantage being an additional $2^1/2$ hours required to reach Lenk.

Instead of crossing Hahnenmoos, bear left and take a footpath leading round the hillside towards the lump of the Regenboldshorn. The path climbs to gain a fairly narrow but grassy pass to the west

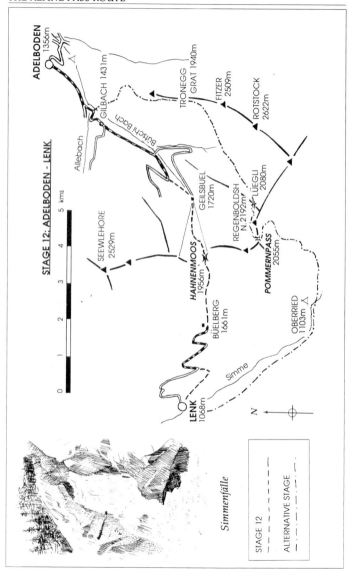

STAGE 12: ADELBODEN - LENK

ADELBODEN 1356m

GILBACH 1431m

Allebach

Bütschli Bach

TRONEGG GRAT 1940m

FITZER 2509m

ROTSTOCK 2622m

GEILSBUEL 1720m

LÜEGLI 2080m

REGENBOLDSH. N.2192m

SEEWLEHORE 2529m

POMMERNPASS 2055m

HAHNENMOOS 1956m

BÜELBERG 1661m

OBERRIED 1103m

LENK 1068m

Simme

N

kms

Simmenfälle

STAGE 12

ALTERNATIVE STAGE

126

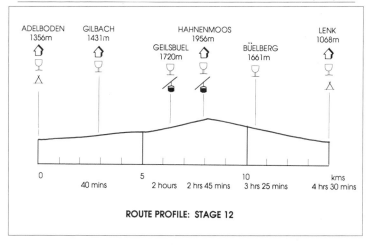

ROUTE PROFILE: STAGE 12

(right) of this peak. This is the **POMMERNPASS** (2055m, about 40 mins from Hahnenmoos). (Given sufficient time and energy, it is worth heading left at the pass and climbing to the summit of Regenboldshorn in 15 minutes. From there the views are particularly fine and worth the extra effort.)

The descent path from the pass veers left and leads over steep pastures, past haybarns and farms, and then takes you through forest. When you come to a junction of paths follow signs for the (1) Simmenfälle. Once you reach this (2 hours from the Pommernpass) cross the walkway in the full spray of the waterfall, and continue down alongside the neatly channelled stream emanating from it - taking care as the rocks can be very slippery - all the way to the valley floor. There you arrive beside a restaurant at the head of the road at **OBERRIED** (1103m; *refreshments*). Buses travel from here to Lenk. A timetable will be found to the left of the restaurant as you arrive.

Note: There is a campsite about 80 metres off to the right.

Walk down the road for about 400 metres, then bear left, cross the river and head to the right on a very pleasant path that takes you to **LENK**.

Main APR: (Hahnenmoos-Lenk)

On the western side of the pass the descent follows an ancient and easy route with grand views across the upper Simmental to the Weisshorn and its neighbouring glacier which comes from the Plaine Morte; views too of the Wildstrubel to the south, but other, greener vistas in the west and out to the north - less grand, perhaps, but no less lovely.

Signposts keep you on the correct route at all junctions. So reach **BÜELBERG** (1661m 3 hours 25 mins; *accommodation, refreshments, bus to Lenk*). From here a minor road winds in long loops down the hillside (short-cuts possible here and there) and at last into **LENK**.

(2) **LENK** (1068m 4 hours 30 mins) *Hotels, gasthofs, camping (at Oberried to the south), shops, banks, PTT, railway (Lenk-Zweisimmen), cable-cars.*

✳ ✳ ✳

Places Visited or Seen on the Way:

1. **SIMMENFÄLLE:** The snows of the Plaine Morte and the Wildstrubel's northern glaciers drain as a number of streams that combine to form the Simme, a river which gives its name to the Simmental. The Truebbach, Laubbach and Ammertenbach all come together below the Ammertenhorn as one riotous, leaping, crashing, foaming spout. The Simmenfälle is seen where it escapes a rocky confine and is then channelled along a man-made gully, through woods and down into the bed of the upper Simmental. It is a spectacular sight and worth the diversion to experience.

2. **LENK:** A small winter and summer resort nestling in a flat and one-time marshy section of the Simmental, of which it is the highest proper village. The village as seen today dates only from 1878 when it was almost completely destroyed by fire. Not only is Lenk suitable as a base for a walking holiday, there are a number of moderate peaks nearby that offer interesting ascents, among them the Wildstrubel and Wildhorn.

The Blattipass

Lac Léman, journey's end - from Col de Chaude

Distance:	18 kilometres
Time:	6¹/2-7 hours
Start altitude:	1356m *High point:* Pommernpass 2055m
Map:	L.S. 5009 Gstaad-Adelboden 1:50,000
Accommodation:	Lenk - Hotels, gasthof, camping (at Oberried 4 kms to the south)
Transport option:	Bus (Oberried-Lenk)

As an alternative crossing to Lenk this route makes an interesting day's outing in its own right. It avoids the Geilsbach valley and the mechanisation that partly devalues Hahnenmoos, and in their place treads a ridge that overlooks Engstligenalp, then explores a quiet little valley below the Fitzer and Rotstock before climbing to the saddle of Lüegli in order to traverse round Regenboldshorn for the crossing of the Pommernpass. At this pass some lovely views are to be enjoyed before dropping steeply to the Sim- menfälle and the valley walk to Lenk.

By direct contrast to the main route via Hahnenmoos, there are no possibilities for refreshment along the way, and few fresh water supplies either, so fill your bottles before setting out.

❋   ❋   ❋

This route begins at the lower hairpin bend on the road leading to Adelboden, beside the soft drinks factory. The signpost names this as **MINERALQUELLE** (1275m). Walk ahead along a tarmac path/ narrow road in the direction of Hahnenmoos. Where it forks at the river, with a signpost giving both directions to Hahnenmoos, take the left-hand route, gaining height along the road. It winds through pastures, passing farms and chalets, then a footpath on the right allows you to break away steeply up the hillside on a short-cut. Follow this narrow path and its continuations (waymarked and signposted much of the way) with fine views down to Adelboden now far below, and across the valley to the Bunderchrinde.

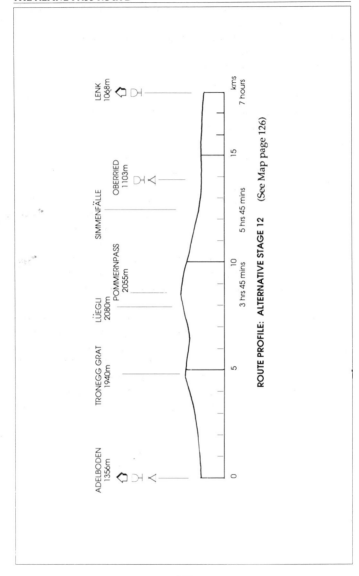

ROUTE PROFILE: ALTERNATIVE STAGE 12 (See Map page 126)

The path eventually joins the road for its final winding to a farm on a grassy ridge, and a little above this farm (Chuenigsbargli, 1739m) you will find a footpath junction giving Hahnenmoos as 2 hours' walk away. Take the path going straight ahead to the south, along the right-hand side of the ridge leading beneath a mechanical hoist and towards woods. Pass through the woods and emerge on their far side near a small farm building (1802m). The path, in places rather faint here, rises steadily and becomes more prominent before you gain the grassy ridge once more at **TRONEGG GRAT** (1940m). There are some delightful views across the head of the Engstligental to a great scoop of pastureland, the Engstligenalp, its waterfalls and the snow-fields of Wildstrubel above. Ahead can be clearly seen the Regen-boldshorn and the large saddle of Hahnenmoos.

Continue up the ridge. The path then begins its steady descending traverse of the western slopes of Fitzer (2509m); first through much vegetation, then across screes, making towards the valley floor. Once down, walk up-valley along the broad track which leads to an upper farm. A waymarked *Bergweg* footpath leads on, climbing roughly south-westwards now to gain a wide grassy saddle at the upper right-hand end of the valley. (Somewhat wild views left to the Rotstock-Ammertengrat crags and corries.)

This saddle is known as **LÜEGLI** (2080m) (not named on the map, but sited between the s and h of Regenboldshorn), with Hahnenmoos given as 30 minutes ahead. The Regenboldshorn looms ahead to the left, and the continuing footpath leads on a traverse of the face of the mountain. Across this take the upper of two paths and you will soon arrive at the **POMMERNPASS** (2055m 3 hours 45 mins). For the descent to Lenk, please consult the route description given under Stage 12, section headed Alternative Route (Hahnenmoos-Lenk).

LENK - LAUENEN - GSTEIG

Distance:	22 kilometres	
Time:	8 hours	
Start altitude:	1068m	*High points:* Trüttlisberg Pass 2038m,
		Krinnen Pass 1659m
Map:	L.S. 5009 Gstaad-Adelboden 1:50,000	
Accommodation:	Lauenen (5 hours 15 mins) - Hotels, gasthof	
	Gsteig - Hotel, gasthof, camping	
Transport option:	Cable-car (Lenk-Betelberg)	

A most enjoyable day's walking with two passes to cross, this stage takes you over a transverse ridge that is pastureland to its very crest, a limestone landscape, rucked and pitted but extravagant with wild flowers during the summer. Trüttlisberg Pass is just far enough away from the main range of Oberland peaks to enable you to gaze on them in a wide sweeping panorama. Then, beyond Lauenen, the wooded Krinnen Pass (or Chrinepass as some maps and signs would have it) presents you with a bold vista dominated by the massif of Les Diablerets. Between the two passes Lauenen adorns a valley green and lush, while Gsteig nestles at the foot of the Col du Pillon which marks the western end of the Bernese Alps. Both Lauenen and Gsteig have much to commend them. They're pretty villages, small and neat and bright with window boxes. Both have two or three well-stocked food stores and, of course, opportunities for refreshment.

It is on this stage that you begin to feel the walk is drawing to a close. The very nature of the mountains is changing. So too the valleys and villages. Not changing for the worse, though. From Lenk to Montreux there are many delights in store, many secrets to be unravelled. If you imagined the magic of the Alpine Pass Route would fade when your back was turned to the Jungfrau, the final two or three days will surely prove you wrong.

Should you feel the need for an easy morning, the Betelberg cable-car is worth considering. It cuts at least two hours from the walking time, saves almost 900 metres of height gain and presents you with a lovely gentle, alternative route to the Trüttlisberg Pass. This section of the route is described below as Alternative Route: (Betelberg-Trüttlisberg Pass).

✻   ✻   ✻

*The route to the Trüttlisberg Pass climbs a long series of ladders
in the woods above Lenk*

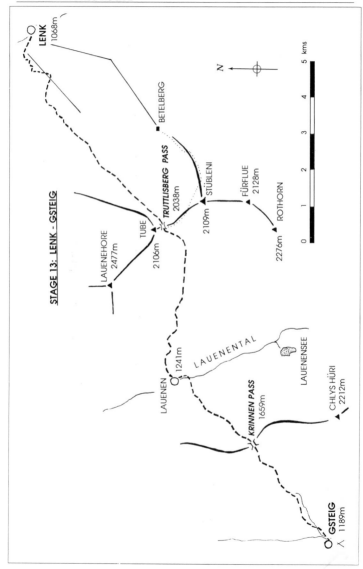

STAGE 13: LENK - GSTEIG

LENK 1068m

BETELBERG

TRUTTLISBERG PASS 2038m

STUBLENI

FÜRFLUE 2128m

ROTHORN

2276m

2109m

TUBE 2106m

LAUENEHORE 2477m

LAUENENTAL

LAUENEN 1241m

LAUENENSEE

KRINNEN PASS 1659m

CHLYS HÜRI 2212m

GSTEIG 1189m

N

5 kms

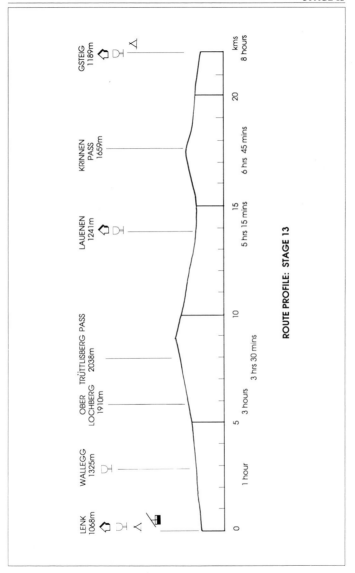

ROUTE PROFILE: STAGE 13

In Lenk's main square, not far from the church, a signpost gives initial directions to the Trüttlisberg Pass. Cross to Hotel Kreuz and continue along the road past it for about 400 metres, then head left on a more narrow road running parallel with the Wallbach stream. This road winds up towards forest, and where it bends to the left you should leave the road and follow a path heading into the trees. The path climbs steeply in forest alongside the stream, then up a series of ladders and stone stairways with waterfalls thundering to one side among chasms of scoured and polished rocks. About one hour after having left Lenk you emerge from the woods to a steep grassy clearing a little above **BERGHAUS WALLEGG** (1325m, *refreshments*). Turn right and walk up the right-hand side of the sloping meadow for about 100 metres, and then take a path breaking away into the woods again. It's a pleasant path at an easy contour, although it gains height a little before taking you across the stream on a sturdy bridge. Not long after this you come out of the woods once more on an enclosed footpath leading to a farm track where you turn left. (There are good views from here looking east to Hahnenmoos.)

The track crosses a rock-strewn streambed and a few paces later you must break away to the right to take a path climbing a rough hillside. (From this point the pass is 1 hour 30 minutes away.) Continue up the path, which can be very muddy in inclement weather, and wander past several isolated farms, the last of which is **OBER LOCHBERG** (1910m 3 hours). All the way now views are quite delightful off to your left, where the larger snow peaks form a crusty rim to the horizon, and the middle ground is one folding ridge after another - a grassy corrugation edged with the dark outline of strips of forest.

Just beyond the farm of Ober Lochberg the way forks. Take the left-hand branch across a stream, and then continue up towards the saddle passing a small hut on the way, and then come onto the **TRÜTTLISBERG PASS** (2038m 3 hours 30 mins) where there is a signpost at a junction of paths.

The first time I came onto this pass two of us sat in the bright August sunshine waiting for a group that never arrived. We idled among the flowers, gazing at hawks on high, at the clear views of mountains we sought to name, scanning each valley and each individual ridge with binoculars, wondering about the sunken limestone pits around us, listening to the insects and the low brush of a breeze among the heavy-headed grasses, the hollow hum of distance which the deaf and the ignorant call silence. Nearly two hours ticked by on our perch in the sun and the group failed to arrive. Shirtless and in shorts I thought I'd found heaven. But a year later we arrived hunched in windproofs. There was a distinct taste of winter in the air, the clouds were heavy and brooding, threatening snow, and it was far too cold to linger. A brief pause and we were off again into the teeth of the wind.

Alternative Route: (Betelberg-Trüttlisberg)
The Betelberg cable-car station is situated near the south-western edge of Lenk and is well signposted. It rises in two stages and you disembark at **LEITERLI** (1943m), the top station. The route to the pass follows an almost horizontal course along a fine ridge, first on one side, then the other. There are grandstand views back to the Hahnenmoos and into the craggy combes of the Wildhorn and Wildstrubel.

On leaving the cable-car take a broad track (signposted to Lauenen) which rounds the first hump to a little col where it continues on the south side of the ridge. The direct route to Lauenen keeps on this side over the Stublenepass (1992m), but a much more interesting (and not much longer) route forks right, signed to Trüttlisberg Pass. The path cuts below the peak of Stubleni above spiny limestone ribs at the head of the Wallbach valley. Mount easily to the rocky ridge which proves to be an exciting tight-rope path among a mass of mini-craters. Pass a small shelter hut and descend left to join the Trüttlisberg Pass route down to Lauenen. (Allow about 1 hour 15 mins from the cable-car to the pass.)

Main APR: (Trüttlisberg Pass-Lauenen)
The way down to Lauenen is straightforward. From the pass bear left and follow a slightly rising path to another junction where you begin the descent proper by dropping down to the right, over pastures and on past a number of farms and barns (VordereTrüttlisberg). The path becomes a track which leads to a metalled road. Turn right. You can either follow this road all the way down to Lauenen in a long series

of loops, or take it for a short distance and then break off at a footpath sign which sends a path down to the left. This path gives a pleasant descent through pastures and small areas of woodland, passing trim chalets on the hillside and eventually, easily, into the village of (1) **LAUENEN** (1241m 5 hours 15 mins; *accommodation, refreshments, shops, PTT, Postbus [to Gstaad], tourist information*).

Turn left and walk through the village towards the head of the valley where the Wildhorn spreads a snowy mantle above the Geltental. About 400 metres outside the main village look out for a signpost directing you onto a meagre path (to Krinnen and Gsteig) which drops on the right to a footbridge over a stream. The route then climbs over meadows and through woodland (very boggy in places), with adequate waymarking and signposts at junctions. In a little under 1½ hours from Lauenen, and without too much effort, you will arrive at the little gap in the wooded ridge which is the **KRINNEN PASS** (1659m 6 hours 45 mins). Directly ahead you gaze over Gsteig's valley to the massif of Les Diablerets, the broad saddle of Col du Pillon and part of tomorrow's route. It is a fine sight.

A little below the pass you reach a farm where the route divides. The main route follows the left-hand path and is shorter and more direct; the right fork adds about 30 minutes to the walk, but is recommended.

Main APR:
Bear left and descend below the farm, soon to come onto a narrow road. Follow this downhill, but keep alert for footpath short-cuts - always worth taking. They lead over meadows and through the woods, and are either marked with signposts or with arrows or waymarks painted on the road and trees. It is an easy, pleasant descent, taking not much more than an hour from the pass. The final stretch is along a quiet valley road that leads past several chalets and brings you onto the main Col du Pillon road opposite Hotel Bähren in the heart of **GSTEIG**.

Alternative Route: (Krinnen Pass-Gsteig)
The right-hand path by the farm leads round among trees, gaining a little height at first, then comes to an open ridge. (If you wander

138

uphill a few paces to the right there are long views to be had over mountains falling away to the north, sliced here and there by hinted valleys. The great slab of the Gummfluh is seen out to the north-west.)

Bear left and descend across a meadow, at the bottom of which you come to a farm. Continue downhill half-left through the centre of another meadow, and steadily lose height among trees and more meadows, finally joining the main route at a narrow road. From here to Gsteig the way is marked almost to excess.

(2) **GSTEIG** (1189m 8 hours) *Hotel, gasthof, camping (about 400m up the road towards Col du Pillon), restaurants, shops, PTT, Postbus (Gsteig-Les Diablerets; Gsteig-Gstaad).*

❊ ❊ ❊

Places Visited or Seen on the Way:

1. **LAUENEN:** A small, modest resort, Lauenen sits amid a pastoral landscape, the Lauenental being gentle and welcoming, but rather marshy to the south of the village. For the backpacker it has a couple of general stores where camping gaz may be bought, plus food supplies. As a base for a centred walking holiday it has much to commend it, with a number of superb outings available from the village. The most popular sight for visitors is the lovely Lauenensee lying below the Geltental. This shallow lake is an idyllic spot, but is unseen from the path of the Alpine Pass Route.

2. **GSTEIG:** Even smaller than Lauenen, Gsteig would also make a first-rate base for a walking holiday. With Les Diablerets rising so grand to the south-west one's attention is naturally focussed there, but there are many other possibilities for good days out whether walking or making modest ascents of the neighbouring peaks. The village has none of the trappings of the larger resorts, and its few shops are mostly general stores with crowded shelves. It has some very attractive houses and a campsite with basic facilities found a short distance away up the Pillon road.

GSTEIG - BLATTIPASS - COL DES ANDÉRETS - COL DES MOSSES

Distance:	23 kilometres
Time:	8 hours 30 mins
Start altitude:	1189m *High points:* Blattipass 1900m
	Col des Andérets 2034m
Map:	L.S. 5009 Gstaad-Adelboden 1:50,000
Accommodation:	La Marnèche (4 hours 20 mins)
	- Berghaus/matratzenlager
	Col des Mosses - Hotels
Transport option:	Postbus/train (Gsteig - Les Diablerets - Montreux)

This penultimate day's walking is visually spectacular from first light until last. There is a steep climb out of Gsteig's valley to begin the day, but then views open out and you wander for hour after hour with an unfolding panorama of beauty to lure you on. The first pass of the day is not even shown on the map. Blattipass is, however, one of the very best viewpoints of the whole walk. From it you can see the extremities of the Bernese Oberland; from the spiky meringue-like tips of the Wetterhorn, past the arrow-shaped Eiger far off, to wave upon wave of snowpeaks running in a long and dramatic line round to the neighbouring slabs and glacial tongues of Les Diablerets.

After Blattipass you plunge into a great bowl of vegetation with the lake of Arnensee gleaming way below. Climbing out again you reach a minor pass looking directly at Les Diablerets, before wandering round to Col des Andérets (more superb views) which gives access to a new valley system (the first of Canton Vaud). For more than three hours you tread a belvedere of delight; a high path linking several remote alps, with wonderful scenes being painted on a magical backcloth right before your eyes. The Dents du Midi are seen, and Mont Blanc shines from afar, peeping between other peaks on other ridges.

At Chersaule you bid farewell to Les Diablerets and all hint of the Oberland, for now you traverse round the end of the long ridge below Pic Chaussy, and just short of the alp of Oudiou begin a forest and pasture walk that leads into the valley of La Raverette. This is all French-speaking country now, and the little resort clustered at the Col des Mosses, the first non-German speaking village since leaving Sargans.

It's a grand day's walking, but it can also be a dry one. Water bottles should be filled before you leave Gsteig. Campers should note that although the map shows a campsite symbol at Col des Mosses, this refers only to a caravan site. There's no official camping ground for tents along this stage, but by continuing for a further 2 kilometres along tomorrow's route, you will come to a campsite beside the road. (See route description below under Stage 15.)

❊   ❊   ❊

From the centre of Gsteig walk north along the road (down-valley towards Gstaad) for a short distance until just beyond Hotel Viktoria where a signpost directs you left onto a short track going to a farm. (Direction of Vorder Wallig, Arnensee, Seeberg and Col du Pillon.) On coming to the farm find a narrow grassy path behind a barn, climbing to a minor farm road where you turn right. After about 100 metres go left on a continuing path heading up through a meadow to rejoin the road again. Follow the road off to the right. After a while this becomes a track and you continue along it until reaching a barn with a signpost pointing left to another path climbing steeply up a meadow bounded by trees. It's a long hard climb and it leads above the meadow, through a dense jungle of raspberry canes and into a lovely grove of fir trees with teasing views ahead of Les Diablerets, and below to Gsteig.

Another steep meadow takes you to the farm of **SCHOPFI** (1502m) perched high on a hillside and looking directly across the valley towards the Krinnen Pass crossed yesterday. From the farm a vague grassy path climbs through more pastures, still steeply gaining height, but with glorious views to compensate for the hard work involved. You will come to a scattering of farms and barns at **VORDER WALLIG** (1716m 1 hour 30 mins). The route continues uphill, and as you gain a hillside shelf so you join a track which now contours comfortably round the hillside to the solitary alp of **TOPFELSBERG** (1814m).

Continue along the track heading south. It soon becomes a narrow path climbing in long twistings to reach the panoramic saddle of the

141

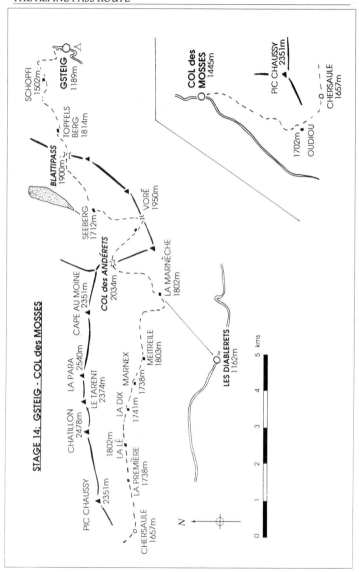

STAGE 14: GSTEIG - COL des MOSSES

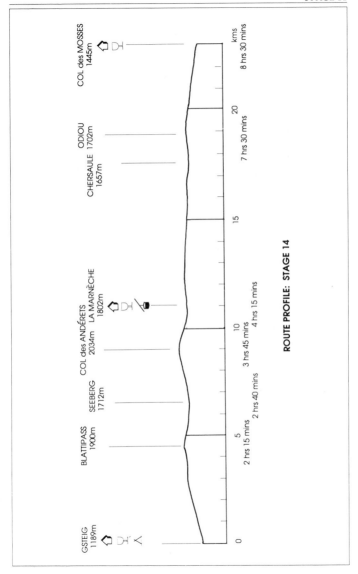

ROUTE PROFILE: STAGE 14

143

Tarn below Voré

BLATTIPASS (1900m 2 hours 15 mins). This is a remarkable place, a grass and shrub-covered ridge punctuated with a few trees, but with a truly memorable view off to the east. It is one of the loveliest and most scenic passes of the whole route. Allow yourself time to absorb it.

When you can tear yourself away descend leftwards on the western side of the ridge, over grass slopes and dodging in and out of trees. In 10 minutes pass the lone building of **OBER STUEDLI** (views down to the Arnensee), and continue on a clear path over pastures, across a pretty stream and onto a track leading to the farm of **SEEBERG** (1712m 2 hours 40 mins) which occupies a delightful site on the hillside, also overlooking the lake of Arnensee. There is a junction of paths here. Leaving the farm below to your right take the path climbing among alpenroses, juniper and bilberries, in the direction of Col du Pillon. Larch and rowan stub the hillside and there are fine views down to the lake far below.

At the head of the slope go through a grass-carpeted col and enter a shallow basin of pasture unlike anything yet seen on the APR. Views ahead are to the snows of (1) Les Diablerets. Cross the basin above a small tarn and reach another col with a drystone wall running across it. This is **VORÉ (CHALET VIEUX;** 1950m 3 hours 30 mins) where there is yet another junction of paths. Here you leave the Bernese Alps and enter Canton Vaud.

Bear right on the route to Col des Andérets, and soon pass the farm of Chalet Vieux to find a road leading ahead. Walk along this road (more distant views to capture the Eiger on the far horizon) to reach **COL DES ANDÉRETS** (2034m 3 hours 45 mins).

Continue to follow the road as it swings round the hillside with views opening ahead that now include the Dents du Midi. Suddenly you realise that the Lake of Geneva is not so far away, for it is the sight of the Dents du Midi that captures the attention of travellers journeying along the lakeside from Lausanne.

The road goes between the alp buildings at **ISENAU** (1855m), and soon beyond these you come to **LA MARNÉCHE** (1802m 4 hours 15 mins; *accommodation, refreshments, gondola lift down to the village of Les Diablerets*). This is the only opportunity for refreshments on this stage of the walk. The road winds to one side of the little hamlet and soon comes to a junction below it. Here you will see a narrow track/path off to your right. Leave the road and walk along the track which soon leads to a lone farm settled into the knuckle of the valley at 1686 metres. Continue past the farm on a path which crosses a stream and then begins to make a rising traverse of the north side of the valley, and in a further thirty minutes comes to the alp of **MEITREILE** (1803m).

The way from here to Col des Mosses is a true belvedere of a path, remaining high above the valley and with splendid views to enjoy practically every step of the way. There is still a long way to go, but it's mostly along a fairly regular contour, just a few ups and downs, the path faint in places, broad and clear in others. Set your mind in neutral and enjoy just swinging along, listening to the cowbells, the tinkle of streams, the sigh of the summer breeze.

The way drops a little to the alp **MARNEX** (1738m), beyond which a clear track leads round to **LA DIX** (1741m), a tight huddle of buildings. Now you can see Mont Blanc to the left of Dents du Midi, and all around - as ever - the great sweep of mountains is superb. After La Dix the track becomes a path again, much trodden by cows, but shortly before reaching **LA PREMIÉRE** (1738m) you come onto a farm road. Follow this for about 1.5 kilometres to the small collection of farms and chalets of **CHERSAULE** (1657m) on a shoulder of mountain where the road curves sharply to the left and begins to descend. Leave the road here and head to the right between the buildings.

We had set out late from Gsteig, been delayed on the Blattipass by our inability to drag ourselves from its fabulous view, and despite the distance we had to cover, had found it almost impossible to respond to any sense of urgency in the day. After several days of poor rain, low cloud and numbing cold winds, Gsteig had presented us with a full moon and subsequent return to summer. So we dawdled with the views, giving ourselves to them, absorbing all the gifts the mountains had on offer. As a consequence we were only at Chersaule when Les Diablerets caught the glory of alpenglow and shadows of night gulped from the valleys.

Yellow waymarks lead the continuing path through Chersaule and on into woods with fine views through the trees. Leaving the woods you walk towards an alp squat upon a clearing on a spur of hillside. This is **OUDIOU** (1702m 7 hours 30 mins). Do not walk as far as the farm but go through a gate on the right to face a new valley - that of La Raverette, with Col des Mosses at its far end. Through the gate head half-left down towards more woods where again a clear path takes you through. *(Wild raspberries to gorge in September, and rosebay willowherb full of tufts of white down wafting in a light breeze, dancing in shafts of morning sunlight.)*

The path brings you to a track which you follow downhill to a minor road. This takes you along the hillside overlooking neat chalets and close-shaved meadows and comes to **COL DES MOSSES**.

(2) **COL DES MOSSES** (1445m 8 hours 30 mins) Hotels, restaurants, shops, PTT, Postbus (Col des Mosses-Chateux d'Oex/train to Montreux).

✳   ✳   ✳

Places Visited or Seen on the Way:
1. **LES DIABLERETS:** A large mountain massif and the last of the

Bernese Alps, it has a number of summits, the highest being 3109m. On the northern side it is strung about with cableways, and throughout the year the upper snowfields and glaciers are skiable. The name Les Diablerets also refers to the scattered village lying deeply below, on the western approach to Col du Pillon in the region known as Ormont-Dessus.

2. **COL DES MOSSES:** A broad open plateau at the head of two valley systems, the col has been developed as a small resort with a cableway rising in two stages to Pic Chaussy to the south-east, and several ski tows on the western slopes. The food stores here are open on Sundays.

COL DES MOSSES - COL DE CHAUDE - MONTREUX

Distance:	28 kilometres
Time:	8 hours
Start altitude:	1437m　　　*High point:* Col de Chaude 1621m
Map:	L.S. 262 Rochers de Naye 1:50,000
Accommodation:	La Lécherette (30 mins) - Camping
	Sonchaux (6 hours) - Pension/matratzenlager
	Montreux - Hotels, pensions, Youth Hostel, camping
Transport options:	Postbus/train (Col des Mosses-Chateau d'Oex/Montreux)
	Train (Caux-Montreux)

The long walk ends on a high note. True, the lofty snow-capped mountains have been left behind, but there's nothing second-rate about the scenery through which this final stage leads. It is constantly varied and consistently lovely. Some of the valleys are exquisite; deeply carved, their walls rising in steep forested slopes to ribs of bleached limestone. One holds a man-made lake with meadows folding gently to the water's edge. Another is protected as a Nature Reserve, with wonderful natural gardens adorned with rowan and beech growing among white boulders and tinkling streams. Architecturally the little farms of the Vaudois Alps are very different from those of the Oberland and farther east, and as you approach Montreux there are extravagant hotels and spa buildings perched on a riviera-like slope above Lac Léman.

It's another long day's walking, almost equally shared between the approach to the pass and the steep descent to Montreux. It's difficult to say which is the more tiring. Both uphill and downhill are demanding in places, but after two weeks of trans-Alpine trekking there's nothing here that you won't be able to take in your stride.

✵　　✵　　✵

From Col des Mosses walk north along the main road (direction Chateaux d'Oex and La Lécherette) for a little over 2 kilometres until you come to a campsite sign on the left, just short of La Lécherette. Walk through the campsite and continue along a path heading

148

*On the final stage to Montreux the APR takes you alongside
the dammed lake of l'Hongrin*

through a corner of woodland, and out across pastures to pass to the
left of a lone farm. The path crosses more meadowlands and leads to
a road about 400 metres west of La Lécherette. Turn left and walk
along this road for about 250 metres. Here you will find a minor road
breaking away half-right ahead. It is a military road, but access is
usually permitted.

Wander along the minor road. It takes you through a modest gorge
and then reaches the eastern end of the reservoir of (1) Lac de
l'Hongrin. A track continues ahead along the right-hand (northern)
bank and, after passing a few houses, comes to another minor road
at **COLONDA JEUR** (1306m). It's a pleasant walk alongside the lake,
the trees growing on promontories above the water throwing reflec-
tions on a clear day; sailboards skimming to and fro and water fowl
congregating at the edges.

Follow the road westwards to the **BARRAGE de l'HONGRIN**
(1257m 2 hours 15 mins), which is situated a little over half-way along

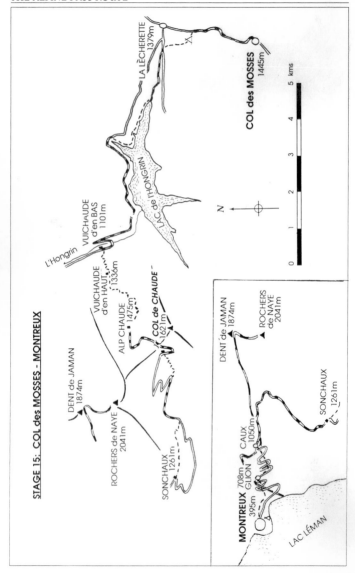

STAGE 15: COL des MOSSES - MONTREUX

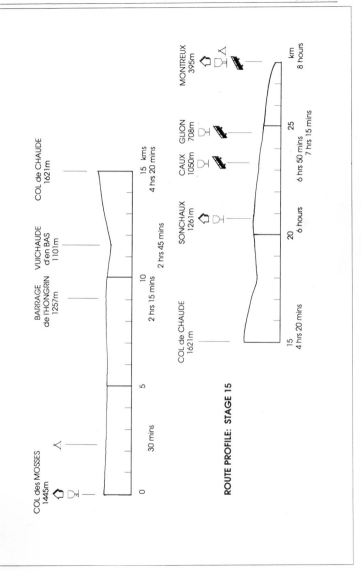

COL des MOSSES
1445m

COL de CHAUDE
1621m

BARRAGE
de l'HONGRIN
1257m

VUICHAUDE
d'en BAS
1101m

0

30 mins

5

2 hrs 15 mins

10

2 hrs 45 mins

15 kms
4 hrs 20 mins

COL de CHAUDE
1621m

SONCHAUX
1261m

CAUX
1050m

GLION
708m

MONTREUX
395m

15
4 hrs 20 mins

20
6 hours

25
6 hrs 50 mins
7 hrs 15 mins

km
8 hours

ROUTE PROFILE: STAGE 15

the lake, and then continue ahead on the old road which takes you through a tunnel above a second gorge and out to a view of the fine, deep, steeply-walled Hongrin valley into which you must descend. This valley is a true delight, one of the loveliest of the whole walk. There is no tourist development; just a simple, unspoiled cleft in the steep mountains, and you wander into it following the road which takes you down in an easy swinging style, past grey shingled farms, forest below and slender rock ribs high above.

We strolled down with light hearts, the valley being swamped with champagne-like sunshine, autumn in the leaves extravagant with nature's gold, three buzzards circling in the sky and mewing to one another in their aerial serenade to the sun. Oh happy Sunday; it was a joy to be ambling through such a valley on such a day.

In the valley bottom, where it begins to level out after the long curves down, and about half an hour from the dam, you come to a lone farm on the right-hand side of the road. This is **VUICHAUDE d'en BAS** (1101m 2 hours 45 mins). Here you leave the road by taking to a vague footpath cutting across a large sloping area of pastureland on the left. There are few visible signs of the path to begin with, although there are yellow waymarks on some of the rocks. Then you cross a stream

Vaudois woodstack outside Vuichaude d'en Bas

and the path becomes more evident as you climb towards a steep woodland. On entering the woods the way becomes well-defined (paved in places) and it leads in a series of zig-zags to gain a fair amount of height.

Eventually you come out of the woods and continue up a very steep grass slope to another farm, **VUICHAUDE d'en HAUT** (1336m 3 hours 25 mins), which has some outstanding views overlooking the valley, the surrounding peaks and the lake off to the south-east.

Pass round the left-hand side of the farm and continue on the path as it swings south-westward round the hillside and brings you to a belt of woodland. The path through can be quite muddy in places, but you soon emerge to a delightful inner valley that is protected as a Nature Reserve (no camping, fires etc.). As you wander deeper into the valley, so it becomes ever more beautiful - limestone boulders, little streams, deciduous trees growing singly or in clumps, fruiting shrubs, flowers, birds flitting among the trees. A superb interlude.

The path meanders through, then cuts off to the right, crosses the main valley's stream and arrives in front of a handsome farm sitting comfortably in a great pastoral basin. This is **ALP CHAUDE** (1475m), and from here a private road winds up directly to the Col de Chaude.

Alp Chaude

The last mountain ramparts above Erniaule

Walk up this road which rises with a regular gradient, and pass through a natural gateway in the ridge linking the Rochers de Naye with Pointe d'Aveneyre. This is **COL de CHAUDE** (1621m 4 hours 20 mins), a glorious balcony overlooking the Lake of Geneva more than twelve hundred metres below.

After more than two weeks of walking, this was the first view of journey's end, a gleam of light on a far-distant lake. A steamer sat in the sunlight while mountains that should have been rising from the far shore were fading in the haze. Between the col and the lake shore there was a lot of mountainside to descend. A lot of very steep mountainside, heavily wooded but with narrow paths delving into the woods. And at the bottom of the woods, unseen from here, a bustling town that spelt the end to the walk. It would take us nearly four hours to reach it.

Continue down the road which twists its way to apparent obscurity, but on coming below a couple of buildings (the first to be met on the western side of the col), break away from the road and descend a

154

footpath dropping down to the left. It takes you through rough pastures and among trees, steeply in places, and eventually returns you onto the road at a hairpin bend. Walk down the road, and after about 500 metres you will pass two more buildings below on the left. This is **ERNIAULE** (1212m), and a few paces beyond the road forks. Continue along the upper road (the lower one goes to Villeneuve) until coming to a right-hand bend where a track breaks away to the right, signposted to Sonchaux and Montreux.

Follow this track, passing a rough cheesemaker's hut at the entrance, and shortly after this, a rather fine, sturdy house. The track/ path becomes another of those delightful belvederes, of which the APR has already exierenced two or three, and it carves its way round the wooded hillside. *(Palisades of light slanted through the trees as we scuffed the leaf-litter of numberless generations of beeches. Green woodpeckers laughed in the distance and robins chittered to themselves, as though sharing a private joke. And when they fell silent the only sound to replace them was that of falling leaves as autumn bit once more.)*

The path climbs a little, then comes out of the woods at a farm. A few paces beyond this you reach **SONCHAUX** (1261m 6 hours; *accommodation, refreshments*) at the head of a minor road which goes all the way to Montreux. You walk along this road as far as Caux. It is a surprisingly pleasant walk, much of the way through woods with views between the trees as the hillside continues to plunge steeply, yet the road winds at an easy contour.

On reaching **CAUX** (1050m 6 hours 50 mins, *refreshments, funicular to Montreux*) continue along the road for a short distance, then take a concrete stairway descending on the left; over a road and down a tarmac path (*Chemin du Tremblex*) signposted to Glion. Cross the railway and continue down. The path takes you through more woods, crossing and recrossing the road. It is an obvious path, the route to Glion being surprisingly rural, but once you reach **GLION** (708m 7 hours 15 mins; *refreshments, funicular*) you must revert to roadwalking for a short distance.

Walk on the right-hand side of the road going downhill and keep alert for an insignificant-looking set of steps marked as *Sentier du Télégraphe,* breaking off to the right. Go down these steps - there are many hundreds of them - leading through trees nearly all the way, for

Montreux, jouney's end

they offer the best pedestrian route to Montreux. On the way down a sudden glimpse is given of Montreux railway station.

As you wander down the last few metres of this epic walk, so the thunderous roar of traffic on a motorway offers a sobering alternative to the many days you've spent within the sound of cowbells and mountain streams.

Finally, at the foot of the steps, walk ahead along Ruelle du Chauderon. At the end of this cobbled street turn right and wander towards Hotel du Pont and continue along the Rue du Pont. Follow this directly to MONTREUX railway station.

(2) **MONTREUX** (395m 8 hours) *Hotels, pensions, Youth Hostel, camping, shops, banks, PTT, railway (links with Lausanne/Paris via TGV; Geneva, for airport etc.).*

✳   ✳   ✳

Placed Visited or Seen on the Way:

1. **LAC de l'HONGRIN:** The lake was established in the 1960s when a large dam was built to generate electricity for the citizens of Montreux. A huge notice-board beside the dam gives a detailed explanation for those who hunger for such technical information. Of a more aesthetic nature, the lake makes a lovely sight with its cradling mountains sending down soft pastures to the waterside.

2. **MONTREUX:** Situated on the south-eastern shore of Lac Léman, Montreux has been a noted resort for two hundred years and more. It was on the itinerary of many European travellers undertaking the Grand Tour during the 18th and 19th centuries, the romantic Castle of Chillon being the main focus of attention. Byron, Shelley, Dumas, Flaubert, Hugo, Dickens all came here, but long before them the site of the castle was occupied in the Bronze Age and later by the Romans. Much of the modern town is both attractive and interesting, although like many European cities it has its surfeit of high-rise blocks that seem sorely out of place. Yet its position on the lakeside is a most forgiving feature.

Cheesemaker's mule

157

APPENDIX A
Useful Addresses

1: Tourist Information Offices:

Swiss National Tourist Office
Swiss Centre
New Coventry Street
London W1V 8EE

250 Stockton Street
San Francisco
CA 94108

104 South Michigan Avenue
Chicago
Il 60603

P.O. Box 215
Commerce Court
Toronto
Ontario
M5L 1E8

608 Fifth Avenue
New York
NY 10020

Verkehrsverband Berner Oberland
(*Tourist Office for the Oberland region*)
Jungfraustrasse 38
CH 3800 Interlaken
Switzerland

Verkehrsverband Zentralschweiz
(*Tourist Office for Central Switzerland*)
Pilatusstrasse 14
Postfach
CH 6002 Luzern 2
Switzerland

Verkehrsverband Ostschweiz
(*Tourist Office for Eastern Switzerland*)
Verkehrsburo der Stadt St Gallen
Bahnhofplatz 1a
Postfach
CH 9001 St Gallen
Switzerland

Office du tourisme du canton de Vaud
(*Tourist Office for Canton Vaud*)
Av de la Gare 10
case postale
CH 1002 Lausanne
Switzerland

2: Other Useful Addresses in Switzerland:

Schweizerischer Camping und
Caravanning-Verband
(*Swiss Camping & Caravan Association*)
Habsburgstrasse 3
CH 6004 Lucerne

Schweizerischer Bund für
Jugendherbergen
(*Swiss Youth Hostels Association*)
Postfach 3229
CH 3001
Berne 22

Verband Schweizer Campings
(*Swiss Camping Association*)
Im Sydefadeli 40
CH 8037
Zurich

3: Map Suppliers:

McCarta Ltd
22 Kings Cross Road
London WC1X 9DS

The Map Shop
15 High Street
Upton-upon-Severn
Worcs WR8 0HJ

Edward Stanford Ltd
12-14 Long Acre
London WC2

Rand McNally Map Store
10 East 53rd Street
New York
NY

Swiss topographical maps are also available from National Tourist
Offices.

Traditional house in Lintal

APPENDIX B
Bibliography

1: General Tourist Guides:

Of the many general guides on the market, perhaps the best and most comprehensive is:

Blue Guide to Switzerland by Ian Robertson (A & C Black, London. W.W.Norton, New York. Published in 1987 [4th edition])

Also useful is *Off the Beaten Track - Switzerland* (Moorland Publishing Co - Ashbourne. Published 1989)

Long out of print, but available on special request from public libraries, the following general guide contains several references to mountain country away from roads and tourist haunts, and gives some interesting background information, although it was written long before the Alpine Pass Route came into being:-

The Alps by R.L.G.Irving (Batsford, London 1939)

2: Mountains & Mountaineering:

There are numerous volumes dedicated to mountaineering in the Alps that contain items of interest to walkers tackling the APR. The list is merely a small selection, but there should be plenty of reading contained within it to provide a background introduction and to whet the appetite for a forthcoming visit.

Wandering Among the High Alps by Alfred Wills (Blackwell, London. Latest edition published 1939) Wills' account of his ascent of the Wetterhorn marked the start of the Golden Age of Mountaineering.

The Playground of Europe by Leslie Stephen (Longmans, London 1871. Other editions followed. Most recent edition, Blackwell, Oxford 1936. In the USA published by New Mountaineering Library, New York 1940) Victorian adventures, including ascent of the Jungfrau. This book is considered to be one of the finest in mountaineering literature.

The White Spider by Heinrich Harrer (Latest edition published by Granada, 1983) History of the North Face of the Eiger by one who made its first ascent in 1938.

The Eiger by Dougal Haston (Cassell, London 1974) History of the Eiger, including modern routes up to the time of publication, by one of the team who made the first direct ascent of the North Face in winter.

The Mountains of Switzerland by Herbert Maeder (George Allen & Unwin, London 1968) Large format book with splendid illustrations. Includes several mountain areas traversed by the APR.

3: Mountain Walking:

The Bernese Alps by Kev Reynolds (Cicerone Press - in preparation) This covers all the areas of the Oberland traversed by the APR, and could be useful for trekkers interested in making diversions, or when taking days off from the main route to explore adjacent areas.

Central Switzerland by Kev Reynolds (Cicerone Press - in preparation) Another guidebook for walkers in the same series as The Bernese Alps. Some of the areas traversed by the APR east of the Oberland are included in this book, and could be useful for offering 'days-off' explorations.

The Titlis heads a range of spectacular peaks, seen from Engstlenalp

APPENDIX C
Glossary

The following glossary lists a few words likely to be found on maps, in village streets or in foreign-language tourist information leaflets. It is no substitute for a pocket dictionary, but hopefully will be of some use.

German	French	English
Abhang	pente	slope
Alp	haut pâturage	alp
Alpenblume	florealpe	alpine flower
Alpenverein	club alpin	alpine club
Alphutte	cabane, refuge	mountain hut
Auskunft	renseignements	information
Aussichtspunkt	belle vue	viewpoint
Bach	ruisseau	stream, river
Bäckerei	boulangerie	bakery
Bahnhof	la gare	railway station
Berg	montagne	mountain
Bergführer	guide de montagne	mountain guide
Berggasthaus	hotel en haut	mountain inn
Bergpass	col	pass
Bergschrund	rimaye	crevasse between glacier & rock wall
Bergsteiger	alpiniste	mountaineer
Bergwanderer	grimpeur	mountain walker
Bergweg	chemin de montagne	mountain path
Blatt	feuille	map sheet
Brücke	pont	bridge
Dorf	village	village
Drahtseilbahn	télépherique	cable-car
Ebene	plaine or plan	plain
Feldweg		meadowland path
Fels	rocher	rock wall
Ferienwohnung	appartement de vacances	holiday apartment
Fussweg	sentier or chemin	footpath
Garni		hotel with meals optional
Gasthaus or gasthof	auberge	inn, guest house
Gaststube	salon	common room
Gefährlich	dangereaux	dangerous
Gemse	chamois	chamois

162

Geröllhalde	éboulis	scree
Gipfel	sommet, cime	summit, peak
Gletscher	glacier	glacier
Gletscherspalte	crevasse	crevasse
Gondelbahn	télécabin	gondola lift
Grat	arête	ridge
Grüetzi	bonjour	greetings
Kamm	crête	crest or ridge
Kapelle	chapelle	chapel
Karte	carte	map
Kirche	église	church
Klamm	gorge, ravin	gorge
Klumme	combe	combe or small valley
Landschaft	paysage	landscape
Lawine	avalanche	avalanche
Lebensmittel	épicerie	grocery
Leicht	facile	easy
Links	á gauche	left (direction)
Matratzenlager	dortoir	dormitory
Moräne	moraine	moraine
Murmeltier	marmot	marmot
Nebel	brouillard	fog, low cloud, mist
Nord	nord	north
Ober	dessus	upper
Ost	est	east
Pass	col	pass
Pension	pension	simple hotel
Pfad	sentier, chemin	path
Pickel	piolet	ice axe
Quelle	source, fontaine	spring
Rechts	á droite	right (direction)
Reh		roe deer
Rucksack	sac à dos	rucksack
Sattel	selle	saddle, pass
Schlafraum	dortoir	bedroom
Schloss	château	castle
Schlucht	ravin, gorge	gorge
Schnee	neige	snow
See	lac	lake
Seil	corde	rope
Seilbahn	télépherique	cable-car

Sesselbahn	télésiège	chair-lift
Stausee	réservoir	reservoir
Steigesen	crampons	crampons
Steinmann	cairn	cairn
Steinschlag	chute de pierres	stonefall, falling rocks
Stunde(n)	heure(s)	hour, hours
Sud	sud	south
Tal	vallée	valley
Tobel	ravin boisé	wooded ravine
Touristenlager	dortoir	dormitory, simple tourist accommodation
Über	via, par-dessus	via, or over
Unfall	accident	accident
Unterkunft	logement	accommodation
Verkehrsverien	office (bureau) du tourisme	tourist office
Wald	forêt, bois	forest
Wanderweg	sentier, chemin	footpath
Wasser	eau	water
Weide	pâturage	pasture
West	ouest	west
Wildbach	torrent	torrent
Zeltplatz	camping	campsite
Zimmer	chambres	bedroom
- frei		- vacancies

Oberland cheese stores at Gschwantenmad

ROUTE SUMMARY

CICERONE GUIDES

Cicerone publish a wide range of reliable guides to walking and climbing in Europe

FRANCE
TOUR OF MONT BLANC
CHAMONIX MONT BLANC - A Walking Guide
TOUR OF THE OISANS: GR54
WALKING THE FRENCH ALPS: GR5
THE CORSICAN HIGH LEVEL ROUTE: GR20
THE WAY OF ST JAMES: GR65
THE PYRENEAN TRAIL: GR10
TOUR OF THE QUEYRAS
ROCK CLIMBS IN THE VERDON

FRANCE / SPAIN
WALKS AND CLIMBS IN THE PYRENEES
ROCK CLIMBS IN THE PYRENEES

SPAIN
WALKS & CLIMBS IN THE PICOS DE EUROPA
WALKING IN MALLORCA
BIRDWATCHING IN MALLORCA
COSTA BLANCA CLIMBS

FRANCE / SWITZERLAND
THE JURA - Walking the High Route and Winter Ski Traverses

SWITZERLAND
WALKS IN THE ENGADINE
THE VALAIS - A Walking Guide
THE ALPINE PASS ROUTE

GERMANY / AUSTRIA
THE KALKALPEN TRAVERSE
KLETTERSTEIG - Scrambles
WALKING IN THE BLACK FOREST
MOUNTAIN WALKING IN AUSTRIA
WALKING IN THE SALZKAMMERGUT
KING LUDWIG WAY

ITALY
ALTA VIA - High Level Walkis in the Dolomites
VIA FERRATA - Scrambles in the Dolomites
ITALIAN ROCK - Selected Rock Climbs in Northern Italy
CLASSIC CLIMBS IN THE DOLOMITES

OTHER AREAS
THE MOUNTAINS OF GREECE - A Walker's Guide
CRETE: Off the beaten track
Treks & Climbs in the mountains of RHUM & PETRA, JORDAN
THE ATLAS MOUNTAINS

GENERAL OUTDOOR BOOKS
LANDSCAPE PHOTOGRAPHY
FIRST AID FOR HILLWALKERS
MOUNTAIN WEATHER
MOUNTAINEERING LITERATURE
SKI THE NORDIC WAY
THE ADVENTURE ALTERNATIVE

CANOEING
SNOWDONIA WILD WATER, SEA & SURF
WILDWATER CANOEING
A CANOEIST'S GUIDE TO NORTHERN ENGLAND (East)

CARTOON BOOKS
ON FOOT & FINGER
ON MORE FEET & FINGERS
LAUGHS ALONG THE PENNINE WAY

Also a full range of guidebooks to walking, scrambling, ice-climbing, rock climbing, and other adventurous pursuits in Britain and abroad

CICERONE

Other guides are constantly being added to the Cicerone List.
Available from bookshops, outdoor equipment shops or direct (send for price list)
from CICERONE, 2 POLICE SQUARE, MILNTHORPE, CUMBRIA, LA7 7PY

Printed by Carnmor Print & Design,
95/97, London Road, Preston, Lancashire.